The Living Vote

Voting reform is the biggest issue of our time. Get that and everything changes

The Living Vote

Voting reform is the biggest issue of our time. Get that and everything changes

David John Allen

BOOKS

Winchester, UK
Washington, USA

JOHN HUNT PUBLISHING

First published by O-Books, 2023
O-Books is an imprint of John Hunt Publishing Ltd., 3 East St., Alresford,
Hampshire SO24 9EE, UK
office@jhpbooks.com
www.johnhuntpublishing.com
www.o-books.com

For distributor details and how to order please visit the 'Ordering' section on our website.

Text copyright: David John Allen 2022

ISBN: 978 1 80341 315 0
978 1 80341 316 7 (ebook)
Library of Congress Control Number: 2022942938

All rights reserved. Except for brief quotations in critical articles or reviews, no part of this
book may be reproduced in any manner without prior written permission from the publishers.

The rights of David John Allen as author have been asserted in accordance with the Copyright,
Designs and Patents Act 1988.

A CIP catalogue record for this book is available from the British Library.

Design: Lapiz Digital Services

UK: Printed and bound by CPI Group (UK) Ltd, Croydon, CR0 4YY
Printed in North America by CPI GPS partners

The author of this book does not dispense medical advice or
prescribe the use of any technique as a form of treatment for
physical, emotional, or medical problems without the advice of a
physician, either directly or indirectly. The intent of the author
is only to offer information of a general nature to help you in
your quest for emotional and spiritual well-being. In the event
you use any of the information in this book for yourself, which is
your constitutional right, the author and the publisher assume no
responsibility for your actions.

We operate a distinctive and ethical publishing philosophy in
all areas of our business, from our global network of authors to
production and worldwide distribution.

Contents

Our democracy is an illusion. Governments are too powerful, and the electoral system is fixed so that nothing can change. This book describes a system that democratises Parliament, constrains the employment of absolute power and significantly improves the relationship between your vote and the exercise of Parliamentary authority.

Change this and everything changes.

Introduction

This book is about protecting our freedom and democracy. To achieve that we need to bring the democratic process closer to the people by changing the structure of the UK House of Commons, and the electoral mechanism we should adopt to populate it. It is not about House of Lords Reform or other constitutional issues, though these also need to be addressed.

The problem is that governments have too much power which is wielded indiscriminately and sometimes unlawfully.[1] Every aspect of our lives can be changed on the say so of one person, with nothing being sacrosanct, nothing off the table. In 2020 and 2021, we saw innocent people effectively imprisoned in their own homes, businesses closed, the elderly isolated, and all it took was a simple diktat. Around the world, we saw draconian measures against an innocent and healthy population. Once again, with little or no debate, little or no discussion, and in all cases no opposition. We've engaged in disastrous wars in Iraq and Afghanistan where false terrors were fabricated in order to convince a supine parliament to agree and to elicit public support.

However, this is just the tip of the iceberg. I will describe how our democracy is actually an elected dictatorship with our only choice being to decide which dictator rules for the next parliamentary period. Sometimes that power is limited by coalitions, but as I will demonstrate, they can lead to even worse outcomes because of egos, ideology, and self-interest. The reality is that coalitions are just a less effective way of achieving the dictatorial power that majority governments, as we understand them now, desire above all else.

Our current system has a very high bar. By that I mean elected representatives need a great deal of support to be elected. Each constituency is an independent election in its own right and the

1

winner takes all. It's called 'First Past the Post' (FPTP). To win a seat under this system a candidate has to get more votes than all other candidates and all the other candidates lose, even if the second placed candidate has only one vote less than the winner. Its downside is that most of the votes cast are ineffective, it is extremely unfair and the resultant government always has minority support.

One solution to the under-representation the FPTP system creates would be to employ one of the many systems under the generic description of Proportional Representation, which has many variations, some of which are in use in other forms of UK election such as the Welsh Assembly and the Scottish Parliament. A major downside of PR systems is that the overall election winner will not likely gain a majority in Parliament and will need to arrange a coalition with another party to be able to govern. As shown with the 2010 coalition between the Conservatives and the Liberal Democrats, they can work well and be better than the dictatorial nature of governments created by the FPTP system. Although coalition government with a proportional voting system would be a good objective, the system I propose here is stronger and gives more control without the drawbacks.

As I will describe later, the British people don't like the idea of messy coalitions that can provide excuses for politicians to abandon election promises, and as any change of system will probably be subject to a referendum, getting the people on-board is essential.

The mechanisms described in this book are designed to remove the dictatorial power of the government yet allow a 'majority' government to be established for the purposes of governance. What the executive will not automatically have, is a majority in Parliament. The system this book describes will enable this new relationship between government and Parliament whilst dramatically increasing representation without the need for coalitions. No other proportional system can achieve this. Far more people will get the MP they voted for, the constituency connection will be stronger, *and each person's vote will live on throughout the entire parliament.*

Make no mistake, government wields enormous power, and even when that power cannot be exercised so easily, they have the unlimited resources to create a justification, to paint a false picture for the purposes of achieving popular agreement, to flood one's every sense with relentless propaganda. We saw this very effective carpet bombing of a false narrative to elicit support to shut down the UK for two years, force people to stay at home, close businesses, and use extreme coercion to effectively mandate vaccines. We were told that 100s of thousands would die from coronavirus – the ONS revealed that around 17,000 died. We were told we should all test regularly – the test was unreliable and even the inventor of the PCR test said it could not be used for this purpose. We were also told vaccines would stop us catching the disease, becoming very ill and passing it on – we now know that after four vaccinations we can still catch it and spread it, die from it and unexplained mortality occurring after vaccination is becoming an issue.

The intention in highlighting the issues that arose in the Coronavirus pandemic is not to cast any judgement on those acts, but simply to make the point that getting agreement, whether that be from Members of Parliament, or the general public, governments have the resources to convince and persuade. Media, academia, scientists, and politicians can all be manipulated, sometimes bought, so we need something in place to protect the rights of ordinary people, a supra governmental constitution, a charter of rights, where any government's principal responsibility would be to protect that.

However, one step at a time. The establishment of a written constitution and the protections it should embody is the subject of another book, perhaps the next one. The processes described here will improve matters significantly and would remain an essential part of creating governance with limits.

Let me explain one obvious complication about rights and actions.

In general, it should be a fundamental right to be able to go about one's business, without intimidation, harassment or in extreme cases being prevented from doing so unlawfully.

By these means, irritating protestors, like Extinction Rebellion, could be sued for preventing people from undertaking their lawful activities. Costs could be high and would be a deterrent to such unreasonable protests. There would not be a need for the criminal law to be engaged as the civil processes would adequately punish and recompense. The right to protest would be part of the statute of rights, but with the proviso that such actions could not impinge upon the rights of others.

So far so good.

Then we view the Canadian Truckers protests of 2022. Oddly, and probably like most people, I do not support the Extinction Rebellion protestors yet supported the Canadian Truckers. It doesn't matter that I think this way, because many will, and many will have the opposite view, that's not the point. The point is that there is a difference between the two protesting groups. Defining what it is, is the problem. It is the case that some mass action, probably more than a protest, is justifiable. What if the government do not uphold the constitution or the charter of rights, would mass action then become lawful under the charter? What if the government broke the law? Is there ever a justification for revolution? In essence when a government acts unlawfully can others' rights then be suspended?

Within any constitution that protects rights and freedoms there would need to be a mechanism to allow necessary mass protest, or another mechanism that would negate any need to blockade roads, and with the power to overturn unreasonable government diktat.

No mechanism is perfect because when the government has weaponry and an army, revolution is the last resort. Let's never forget the massacre in Tiananmen Square, 4th June 1989. As I write this, Canada is moving perilously close to injuring Canadian citizens, so the actions there have parallels in the past.

Another constitutionally granted right must be access to justice, but for that to happen we would need a revolutionised legal structure with far greater accessibility. Currently, courts are congested, and litigation is too expensive for most people. This needs to improve anyway.

The rights and benefits of people must always trump the self-interest of politicians. Democracy, embodying regular elections, changes the motivations of politicians as their prime objective is to get elected, not to make our lives better. If they can do both, then great, but if one has to suffer it will not be the electoral effort. To balance these swings, to encourage a longer-term view, beyond the next election, the absolute power of the executive, and in particular, the Prime Minister, should be restrained a little. The systems and processes described later will do this, but reform shouldn't end there.

Democracy works. The better we can apply the principles of people power, the better our governance will be. If that weren't true, then what else? The electoral system described in this book will extend representation, reduce the dictatorial power of government, whilst enabling a single party government to function, pretty much as it does now.

After the 2015 general election, I completed work on an idea for voting reform that would better address the need for greater representation of the people in the House of Commons, allowing for more people to get the representative for whom they voted and ensuring that votes cast by MPs in the House of Commons reflected the number of votes received by any particular MP.

The system was (and is) called F2PTP, first two past the post. There is a chapter on my voting reform proposals, including F2PTP, later in the book.

This system is still only a part of the eventual solution because in the intervening period, that time between the development of F2PTP and early in 2022, it has become clearer to me that more needs to be changed. Even though this voting mechanism is still far better in terms of proportionality than FPTP, it fails to solve the underlying problems of a system that has become progressively corrupt and manipulative, as do all regimes eventually. There are groups that support proportional representation (PR) and have campaigned for different versions of PR systems. However, none of these have managed to solve the underlying problems and they could make matters worse. I shall discuss the various merits and demerits of these PR voting systems in a later chapter, but suffice to say, and in my opinion, the people in these groups are strongly wedded to their preferred system and are completely opposed to any notion that theirs might not be the one to adopt. UKIP, though not an electoral force, have already declared an allegiance to Make Votes Matter who are unswerving cheerleaders for STV (Single Transferable Vote).

The two main parties remain firmly in favour of the existing system because it benefits them, the Liberal Democrats are already wedded to STV, as declared in their 2019 manifesto, and the Green Party are also committed to Make Votes Matter, almost as if it is the default position for anyone supporting a more representative voting system.

In Labour's 1997 manifesto, the following appeared:

We are committed to a referendum on the voting system for the House of Commons. An independent commission on voting systems will be appointed early to recommend a proportional alternative to the first-past-the-post system.

It is amazing what a 178-seat majority can do to voting reform promises. You can be certain that neither Labour nor the Conservative party are remotely interested in voting fairness, just winning.

I became interested in the voting mechanisms in 2015 and wanted to devise a system that could garner public support with logical argument, to counter the earlier setback. We had already seen a disastrous referendum on the AV (Alternative Vote) system on 6th May 2011, with the proposal being defeated by a massive 67.9% to 31.1% margin, astronomical in referendum majority terms. Unfortunately, this set the bar far too high for any early repetition of a voting reform referendum.

The excuses given for the astonishing defeat were principally technical. AV really isn't PR (as if anyone knew the difference). If we'd had a proper PR system, etc., when the reality was that it was defeated by two statements but just one argument:

- FPTP realises majority government, which is strong government.
- PR means coalitions, just like that shower over in Europe.

Majority government was defined as being decisive, a government with the power to implement its policies without partisan objections based on political agendas. It's a familiar system, we know how it works and, principally, we know that we can kick out an entire government in one fell swoop. It is a powerful argument. Any system that keeps this as an option will garner support.

In the referendum campaign, people were reminded of the horror stories about Belgium being without a government since 26th April 2010 (it was to continue like this for 589 days), or the never-ending machinations of other European governments struggling with their PR systems and difficult coalitions. In 2011, we also had a coalition government at the time and were beginning to see the downsides of two parties haggling over the right thing to do, and abandoning, in the case of the Liberal Democrats, a cast iron manifesto commitment on student fees that got them many of their seats in the first place. As we know, it all ended in tears.

There was an instinctive dislike of coalition politics by the British people, and I've seen nothing since to change that perspective. The inescapable conclusion is that unless the argument of strong majority government is defeated by a simple to understand and equally powerful concept, then any future attempts to reform our voting system would be met with the same objections.

There were also many peripheral objections to a complicated system where the outcome is not transparent to the voter. All so-called PR systems suffer from this excess of complication and, as a result, nobody understands how they work. More importantly though, they suffer from the coalition monster. Under the same structures we have now, any form of more representative voting will lead to coalition government between parties, and coalitions are abhorred by the people.

The voting system I developed, whilst easy to understand and implement, will still lead to coalition, so I have amended the overall concept to arrive at a mechanism that doesn't rely on coalitions yet retains a significantly better spread of representation. Before going further into this concept, I want to discuss some of the real problems of broad coalitions between parties with quite different views.

In the last couple of years, I've spent a lot of time in Sweden, a country with a very proportional voting system that has eight parties which form the 349 members of the Riksdag (Swedish Parliament). There is also one independent at the time of writing, though only by virtue of leaving the party she was elected for after the 2018 elections. Currently, it has a continuing and fragile coalition between the Social Democrats, who have ruled for decades with the Greens (formerly) and the Left Party, but suffers from a growing presence of conservative parties, in particular the Sweden Democrats, typically labelled as 'far-right', as the left are wont to do to any opposition. Currently, the Sweden Democrats have 62 of the 349 seats in the Swedish Riksdag, but coalitions are difficult to achieve when truly far left parties refuse to cooperate with the Sweden Democrats. This situation will likely become very interesting at the next election later this year (2022) as support for the Sweden Democrats has risen substantially.

Typically, small parties, like the Greens, who have walked out of their coalition because they didn't get what they wanted, have exercised power and influence far beyond their electoral support. Like the UK, Sweden has enormous but very green energy resources, delivered largely by the hugely successful dams in the north, yet is suffering (also like the UK) a massive hike in electricity prices.

The Swedish coalition government is a direct result of their voting mechanism and parliamentary structure, and whilst that remains, meaningful change is difficult to come by. Smaller parties dominate by insisting on closing down nuclear generation for ideological purposes. If your party manages to pass the arbitrary 4% of the national vote barrier then your one or two members may be needed for that all important majority, so ministerial positions await.

Remember how that works? The smaller partner in the last UK coalition managed several ministerial positions and their leader was rewarded with the important sounding, but utterly meaningless title of 'Deputy Prime Minister'. Ministerial positions weren't awarded on merit but on political expediency – and I don't wish to imply that they are awarded exclusively on merit at any other time.

Sweden has a huge immigration problem, entirely self-inflicted. In keeping with left-wing views, their left-wing government has had an open door to immigration, particularly Muslim immigration. The general election in September 2022 is likely to add a new and interesting dimension. A new Islamic party has been formed to contest these elections called Nyanset (Nuance Party). Currently, of Sweden's alarming 20% levels of immigration, those from majority Muslim countries make up over 8%. The Swedish voting system is going to struggle with this option as, if only half of the immigrants from Muslim countries vote for them, parliamentary representation is guaranteed. Were the Nyanset Party to be needed in a coalition, Sweden may be pushed toward Islamic political objectives against the interests of the native Swedes.

The ruling Social Democrats have benefitted from the immigrant vote significantly, so things may just balance themselves out, but the risks are clear.

In the UK, such small levels of representation are meaningless. Support levels upwards of 15% are needed to stand even a chance of election, although the support is counted at constituency level and not national, so high levels of local support can be achieved, where that is only local, when national support is non-existent. Examples are the anomaly of the Brighton Pavilion constituency, held by Caroline Lucas for the Green Party, and areas such as Scotland with a strong nationalist agenda.

The good news is that F2PTP retains this high bar and minority support would not see an Islamic party with ministerial power in the UK, but we need something that will not only secure that objective but also avoid the need for uncomfortable coalitions.

In this outline, it looks as though I've made a pretty convincing argument against changing the voting system, and in a way I have. I would certainly argue now against a system that gave undue power to ideologies that had little support, and all the PR systems that have been, and are currently on show, risk doing that. I would also argue now against a system that required coalitions in order to function, because the very nature of coalitions scream compromise, and may trample on those ideas one holds dear. I also hold as sacrosanct the opportunity to rid oneself of a government immediately, with no half measures. It is a peculiarly satisfying element of the British system, and of those countries that followed suit. The boss of yesterday is the nobody of tomorrow, and we need to keep that. The mechanisms described in this book will significantly increase representation and avoid the need for coalition government.

In summary then, this book is about describing a mechanism to elect a parliament, from which a government will be formed through a system that has the following aspects:

- That more people get the person for whom they voted.
- That voting in the House by MPs will be directly proportional to the votes they received in the election.
- That the government of the day can be unceremoniously sacked by the election.
- That coalitions in order to govern with authority would not be necessary.
- That the voting system is simple and explainable in a single paragraph.

My proposals mean that we can keep all the benefits of the FPTP system yet increase representation and fairness across the board.

I am a firm believer that one needs to know where one is going before planning the route. Well, this is the end objective and the details of how it can work and the benefits to be had are what this book is about.

Note:

1. The judgement on 15th February 2022, by Mr Justice Singh and Mr Justice Swift, against the government, when Matt Hancock was found not to have complied with the 'public sector equality duty', as one example.

Chapter 1

Corruption

Corruption is endemic within our political system and exacerbated by the incentives created by our electoral processes. In this case I'm not talking about theft, or direct bribery, though there are instances coming very close to that, neither am I talking about the use of high office for deliberate personal enrichment, though once again some activities are perilously close. I refer to the exercise of patronage, imposition of loyalty demands, large monetary gifts for parties and individual politicians, post office directorships, etc. The net effect is that elected representatives often vote for things they do not agree with, and this enables a gradual moving away from the rights and freedoms we have come to regard as sacrosanct toward an alternative which is increasingly authoritarian and elitist.

New forms of governance usually begin well, and democracy has survived for longer than other regimes. Of course, living under a benevolent dictator can appear idyllic for a while, but then the mantle passes on, and things can change very quickly. We've reached a stage in the UK where representation is at an all-time low, governments with majorities behave like dictators, opposition is completely powerless regardless of support and consequently focus on points scoring. In Parliament, opposition is toothless. The government dominate in all aspects from committee membership to voting. This leads to hugely dysfunctional debate, which really isn't debate. In order to enhance their chances of success in the next election, opposition parties focus on government mistakes, or individual behaviour, in fact anything but constructive actions. Opposition is also total; one person decides how their entire parliamentary party will vote.

Within the internal committee mechanisms of parliament and away from the gaze of the media and public eye, politicians do work together, and it isn't always the hostile environment we see at PMQs. Despite these deviations from the artificial conflict with one side always against the other side, we do have a polarised political system which increases the polarisation of society in general. I think it would be better, were we to have a legislature that was a little less black and white or left and right on the big issues and I also think there is a way to do this.

Social self-awareness has blossomed in the last 40 years or so. Much of this might have been aided by the Internet and the ease with which we can get information, but there is little doubt that we are more conscious about equality and the value of the individual than in any previous generations. Is it not odd, therefore, that we still prefer to be ruled by our 'betters'?

This is borne out by the background of both the Cabinet and Shadow Cabinet of early February 2022 (these things can change rapidly).

The Conservatives, out of 29 cabinet members, have 13 that went to either Oxford or Cambridge, 3 Eton Boys, and 8 who didn't go to university at all (polytechnics, agricultural colleges, or secondary schools only). For the Shadow Cabinet of 31, the numbers are 11, 0, and 4. There can be little doubt that these people belong to an extremely elite group, and that, ironically, is what people seem to want. Imagine your work colleagues, golfing group, circle of friends, associates, etc. How many of them would you unswervingly support for ministerial office?

People usually want their leaders and legislature to be better than them, by whatever means each person uses to judge that, and selection by a long-standing and well-known political party purportedly offers this security. It is a process that has worked quite well for a considerable period of time. The question is, does it work well now? I don't think so for the following reasons.

The major problem with the make-up of our parliament is that our electoral system means the distilling of opinion in to two camps. When voting locally, but with the outcome deciding the national government, there is no point in supporting alternative parties whose agenda would better fit your own views. Only one of the two parties can win power, and votes are often cast against the one you dislike most as opposed to an endorsement of the party you actually vote for. In the UK we do not have a national election, but 650 local ones, however, the implication of the effect of your vote and the cumulative outcome is clear to all. Oddly there is no formal or statutory body responsible for collating results. We leave that task to the media. The local authority, borough council or unitary authority are charged with all aspects of each local election and from my experience, which is limited, they discharge these responsibilities very well indeed.

The first issue is with how our government is formed regardless of the mechanism of getting people elected, then there is the electoral process itself, which will be discussed in detail in another chapter.

By whatever means our parliament is formed, the end result is often the same, one of the two parties have an overall majority, or a majority over the other main party. Some smaller parties do gain seats in the UK legislature, mostly the nationalist parties of Scotland, Northern Ireland, and Wales, a few for the Liberal Democrats in constituencies where they have been active for a long time, and one for the Green Party, in that quite peculiar constituency (electorally) Brighton Pavilion.

However, regardless of how the votes fall for the two main parties the objective remains the same, to establish a majority government. If overall majority is achieved, as in 2015 and 2019, the control of that party is total. Where an overall majority isn't achieved as in 2010, and 2017, four options exist. One is to form a coalition government as in 2010, another is to enter into a supply and confidence agreement with another party as happened in 2017, and a third is to rule as a minority government. The fourth option is to call another election. Generally, coalition or supply and confidence are chosen. Coalition provides a majority, but with compromise, supply and confidence doesn't provide an automatic majority for everything, but it does for main manifesto commitments.

In 2010, the Conservative Party fell short of the desired overall majority by 19 seats. The Liberal Democrats had 57 seats, so the potential Prime Minister, David Cameron, and the Leader of the Liberal Democrats, Nick Clegg, entered into coalition discussions. The result was an uneasy coalition (as I've already alluded to in an earlier chapter). The welching on a firm manifesto commitment by the Liberal Democrat party to abolish student tuition fees rebounded with catastrophic results for them. In the 2015 general election they returned only 8 seats, a loss of 49, or to look at it another way, they lost 86% of their seats in one election period. Clearly coalitions can be problematic.

Despite the political disagreements of coalition, the 2010 government was quite successful in my view. It worked better than majority government would have done because for the first time in a long time there was greater representation in that government than in majority governments, meaning that a greater proportion of the electorate were represented. All those who supported the Liberal Democrats were effectively added to all those who supported the Conservatives. Bearing in mind that votes for losing candidates are also supportive votes, more of the electorate supported the coalition government of 2010 than would have supported a majority Conservative one.

In 2015, David Cameron achieved a small majority, but resigned after the Brexit referendum defeat. The general rule is that governments win referendums because they have significantly more resources than the opposition. In this case though the government lost, and David Cameron resigned to be replaced by Theresa May. Prime Minister May felt that her majority wasn't sufficient and called another general election in 2017 in which she lost the majority she had by 7 seats. Once again, some form of majority was needed so this time a supply and confidence arrangement was agreed with the DUP (Democratic Unionist Party), a Northern Ireland party, broadly conservative in nature and more or less on the same page as the UK Conservative Party. As is common with these deals a bartering process began in which the DUP extracted a considerable sum of money from the Conservatives to be utilised in Northern Ireland.

Normally a party can rely upon the support of its own people, but the EU withdrawal agreement that Mrs May attempted to pass in Parliament was severely defeated three times by huge majorities. On 23rd July 2019, Boris Johnson became leader of the Conservative Party. On the following Day the Queen accepted the resignation of Theresa May and appointed Boris Johnson as Prime Minister. In October 2019, and due to the lack of a suitable majority in Parliament the Prime Minister called a general election to be held on 12th December 2019, which resulted in a significant Conservative majority of 80.

Interestingly, whilst other smaller parties find it difficult to get elected, entirely due to the voting system and quite detached from electoral support, they can have a dramatic effect on the results of others. The most significant of the 'others' was a new party, led by the former UKIP leader Nigel Farage, sometimes referred to as the 'Father of Brexit'. In 2014 and 2019 UKIP, then The Brexit Party, won the European elections. In 2019, the result was astounding for them. 29 seats out of 59 in total and 5.24 million votes. In the 2015 general election UKIP polled just under 3.9 million votes. Regardless of the name change, people knew very well what UKIP and The Brexit Party stood for and millions supported them.

In 2015 the SNP got 59 seats with 1.4 million votes yet UKIP only 1 seat with 3.8 million votes so the disservice to English voters was disgraceful. To add fuel on that particular fire, Scotland has its own Parliament in addition to the Scottish MPs in Westminster. That the SNP can have such disproportionate representation and influence on English matters is completely unjustifiable.

That disparity remains.

In 2019, Boris Johnson was the Conservative Party leader. He had been a prominent campaigner for Brexit in the referendum and, rightly or wrongly, he was seen as the best option to 'get Brexit done'. That became a campaign slogan, and the result was a huge win for the Conservatives. However, it's not quite as clear cut as it seems. Critical to the huge majority that the Conservatives won, was the decision by Nigel Farage to stand down all The Brexit Party candidates in constituencies where there was a Brexit-supporting Conservative candidate standing. Nowhere was this effect more keenly felt than in the so-called 'Red Wall' seats, predominantly in the North of England. Nigel Farage gave the Conservative Party a free run. I do not think this has ever happened before on such a scale and it has contributed to an almost Brexit, with the sacrificing of Northern Ireland as a part of the UK the most prominent issue.

Just to put things into perspective, every government faces repeated crises. In 2010 it was the economic crash, 2017 and 2019, the EU problem, 2020 and 2021, a declared pandemic and the curtailment of freedoms never before seen outside wartime.

Critical to these recent actions, almost no debate was held regarding the imposition of emergency actions, no accountability on massive spending and corruption in high office and the blatant disregard of isolation rules by those that set them. I'm not suggesting that debate would have eased any of this, because the official opposition has consistently called for greater draconian actions and MPs themselves are quite content to vote the way they are told.

These then are the resultant problems with our parliament:

- Majority government is an elected dictatorship.
- Opposition is simply an opposing dictatorship.
- The chasm between those in power and those without is absolute.
- Our democracy only gives the people the option to change dictators.

Let's look at these claims in more detail.

Our parliament gives the illusion of democracy, but in reality, government policy is dictated by one person, the Prime Minister, and opposition policy is dictated by the leader of Her Majesty's Official Opposition. I don't mean that these individuals design all the policy, far from it, but nothing will happen if they don't agree. An absolute veto is a dictatorship by any other name. It may be that colleagues will apply pressure in one way or another, but the dictatorship still exists. The former Russian Empress, Catherine the Great, a brilliant woman and a great reformer was well aware that her absolute power was entirely dependent upon the support of the nobility and as a result her attempts for constitutional reform, in particular abolishing serfdom, were prevented by them. In a sense our illusory democracy offers even more power to the leaders of majority governments than was enjoyed by kings and emperors of the past. Even if opposition is driven by self-interest, it remains opposition. As MPs are fed by the state, their narcissistic tendencies massaged by the media, and their safety ensured by toeing the line, true opposition is hard to come by.

When people have too much power, they behave badly.

Both the Labour and Tory parties are highly managed organisations. Our electoral system determines that a majority of these local elections, constituency elections and Local Authority elections are always won by one of the two main parties. It doesn't matter how many people oppose them they always win. This is such a reality that when a constituency comes up which is highly likely to go in a known direction, like Southend West (February 2022) for example, a candidate is selected from an approved list. Often, as in this case, the candidate, Anna Firth, who did not live in the constituency, moved there before the vote, showing just how confident they were of winning. Most people simply didn't care and didn't vote with a turnout of only 24%, but this is immaterial in the UK as winning is all that matters, support is irrelevant. The pattern is often repeated. It happened in 2015 with Tom Tugendhat, similarly, moving into the constituency after selection by the Conservative Party but before the vote. The name for this practice is carpetbagging.

In Southend West, the election was also significantly distorted because the Labour Party, the Liberal Democrats and the Greens did not compete, citing a respect for the former MP, David Amess, who was murdered in 2021. However, this is more likely to be an excuse to avoid an election they couldn't possibly win, save money, and display some artificial virtue to boot. If you doubt this just imagine that this seat was deemed to be very winnable by Labour and was the one seat needed to deny the Conservatives a majority, then ask yourself if they would stand down under those circumstances. It's an immoral position to take because it denies people their right to vote for who they want.

The foregone nature of so many constituencies is one major reason why people just don't bother to vote. This is a situation which is exploited by the big parties. When a politician is guaranteed to remain in his position regardless of performance or ability or conflicts of interest, where's the motivation to serve their constituents?

Our parliament is made up largely of career politicians who can't be kicked out (in general). Theoretically, people could vote for anyone, the reality is that they do not. Other seats, which do change hands from time to time, are the determinants of the government. However, the outcome of the election, whoever wins, is the same, A dictator takes charge.

Parties control candidate selection ruthlessly. If there is no chance of winning then the party doesn't care; if there is a good chance or certainty of winning, the party will decide the candidates. Generally, and superficially, this might seem to be a reasonably good way to populate a parliament. These are well educated people, some of them with careers and real work experience (though few with the latter). However, what are the truly important characteristics to get that all important selection, for a winnable seat? Is it innovation, commitment to ideas, fierce defence of one's constituents' rights, always standing up for the right things?

No.

The real winners on your CV include, for example, family connections. Have a father or an uncle as a former MP or donor. If you really want to spend or are in a position to help a beleaguered leader you can avoid elections altogether and become a minister of the crown for the right sort of support. A friendly investigation or a record of substantial donations for example. Be presentable and reliable. Obviously, reliability really means unswerving loyalty (vote the way the whips tell you), public support, even for hopeless cases (partygate), but above all don't rock the boat.

Parliament is full of MPs who have never (or extremely rarely) voted against their government. One might ask, what's the point of electing them? On the one hand, there are substantial punishments for disloyalty, or independent thinking, by way of losing patronage and opportunity.

Surprisingly, whilst the processes of both the major political parties border on immoral and skewed practices, they aren't all bad. Selection based on questionable criteria does maintain a certain standard for candidates; generally, they are well educated and reasonable people and as a screening process it is largely effective. In the changes that I recommend, the party aspect of this will still work in pretty much the same way, but with massive improvements in representation. What's wrong with the legislature now is the dictatorial nature of it and the absence of true representation. Missing in the legislature is the need to gain support from people who owe no loyalty pledge to a party. People who decide issues based upon their own views and therefore act as a temperate measure against dictatorial tendencies.

Whilst in theory the official opposition are supposed to do this, their approach has more to do with positioning for the next election opportunity and they are doomed to oppose for the sake of opposing, forever.

This polarisation artificially generated by our governmental structure makes meaningful change impossible to achieve. Progressively governments are forced out to the perimeters of policy, completely unable to address fundamental issues. The electoral fall-out from touching a political sacred cow would be fanned incessantly by the opposition for electoral advantage. Add to that the nature of the assembly being made up of people who are 'reliable chaps and chapesses' and the end result is almost permanently sterile governance.

In the absence of free thinking and stable structural reforms, much effort is directed to minor adjustments, the most common of these being throwing more money at an already dysfunctional system or structure. Massive argument is inflamed by a partisan press over minor technicalities, fuelling an entirely fabricated divide. The entire system is then sustained by a polarising voting system.

We are not short of societal, social, financial and political problems to solve, but our system simply doesn't allow novel approaches, and our parliament, therefore, ignores those options.

In summary then our legislature is defective because we can only choose between two equally divisive dictatorial processes. This leads to corruption (donors don't give millions for nothing), patronage, bribery, and artificial opposition.

True representation in our current system is extremely narrow.

In terms of choosing our governance the 2019 general election showed that only 17% of votes cast counted towards that. If you consider the total number of registered voters, it's only 11.6%.

82.76% of votes cast (26,495,511) were totally ineffective in achieving this objective.

Is it any wonder that people don't bother to vote?

Chapter Summary.

Governments have total power, oppositions none. They are granted this power with a very small minority of the vote.

This encourages corruption, bribery, self-interest and leads to poor government.

The next chapter:

Explains the many faults of our electoral system and why it leads to bad government.

Chapter 2

The Failure of First Past the Post (FPTP)

As outlined in the last chapter, the way we select a government leads to a dictatorial regime, almost exclusively, masquerading as democracy. The only thing we can do as a people, is to change dictator from time to time, and in between these choices we are ruled by a government and are subject to legislation, sometimes extreme, on the approval of just one person. Periodically we get the chance to choose the same or another government and dictator but give them the same degree of absolute power.

In practice, it is a dictatorship, presented as democracy. The government gets what it wants by virtue of a parliamentary majority. If such a majority isn't returned at the election, they seek to cobble one together, and if that isn't possible a lesser form of parliamentary majority called Supply and Confidence is sought, and if that fails another election may be called as happened in 1974 in the Wilson era.

Our government is dependent upon a majority in Parliament because opposition is polarised. Under our electoral systems, minority governments rarely work because the official opposition is constantly seeking an opportunity to create a situation whereby another election has to be called. In much the same way as the loser of a best of three bet, always wants a best of five. As government is under the direction of one person, so opposition is aggregated under a similar unitary authoritarian. Members of parliament do not vote independently, but in accordance with their party allegiance.

Conservative MPs supporting a Conservative agenda or Labour MPs supporting a Labour agenda is unsurprising. After all, these are long-standing parties, and their campaign territory is well known and designed to be as different as possible for election purposes. Whereas in reality, they all do pretty much the same thing when in power, driven by events and available finance, and there's always a crisis which tends to dictate political direction. To get elected parties must present themselves as being different but often there's very little practical difference in outcomes. From time to time though they can make decisions that affect the lives of people in dramatic ways, and when that happens the absence of effective opposition becomes critical.

Two examples spring to mind.

- The 1914-1918 war was entirely avoidable. We entered a squabble, that was not our concern, and lost three-quarters of a million souls all from our young manhood in this pointless escapade. The surrender conditions and economic devastation foisted on Germany after the war created the ideal breeding ground for extremism and the rise of a political power that would destroy Europe a second time. More recently we have engaged in warfare in Iraq, Afghanistan, Syria and to a lesser extent Libya. In early 2022 the political narrative, unopposed, seems to be preparing people for yet another conflict.
- The Coronavirus pandemic saw the greatest restrictions on civil freedoms outside of wartime conditions. The introduction of emergency legislation became the excuse to shut down an entire country, and these laws remain in place two years later when no emergency existed.

In the first example, the lack of meaningful opposition led to devastating wars; in the second, the continuation of extreme measures long after any real threat had dissipated, again due to an all-powerful state and no effective opposition.

However, the real danger is, ironically, the ineffectiveness of governments to tackle the big issues.

Healthcare is one such issue. It's difficult, perhaps impossible to change because it is a battleground on which the Conservative Party and the Labour Party use for electoral duels. The mantras presented in this most combative of arenas is inaccurate and misleading, but rests upon a public perception that has been developed over many years. The people regard the NHS as the best system in the world when it's not even close. Over recent years is has become even worse, yet designing a healthcare strategy for the future, to meet greater demands, is becoming critically urgent, but the only thing politicians seem to be able to do is throw money at it, or tinker around the edges. Why is that?

Our electoral system, FPTP, artificially creates majority government with total power in Parliament, but with low public support in the country. In order to create the healthcare structures that people need and want, or to just discuss the options, the misplaced devotion to our outdated and hugely dysfunctional NHS needs to be overcome, which in turn requires considerably more trust in the government machine than is possible. If anything, the stock of politicians is about as low as it could get, so weening a dependent and loving populace away from the NHS, even though it is collapsing around us, doesn't seem possible. Whatever the circumstances, it would be challenging, but it isn't even up for discussion, largely because of the fear of providing political opposition a 'nuclear' option in an election campaign. The stark duality, the opposition for the sake of it, is caused by the voting system, which remains because it suits two parties, marginalises everyone else and creates majority government from minority support. Achieving change is so difficult that there isn't even a vision or an outline of what would be needed to satisfy the health demands of an expanding elderly population.

The support element is critical but unseen because opposition makes itself known through other channels. Over the dinner table, down the pub, at the football, on talk shows, demonstrations, and a host of other activities that people engage in to express their views. When a government, and a legislative process has more support, then it is more likely that the politically more difficult subjects could be addressed.

It would help if Parliament as a body could meet this challenge, but as it is such a black and white electoral issue (it's winning, not doing the right thing, which is important to them), it will continue to be propped up and we'll all be the worse for it.

The coalition government of 2010 did have more support than an individual party government could have done, and it embarked upon a difficult strategy of public financial restraint and lasted the whole five years. In that sense, it was successful. Coalitions though bring other problems which we need to avoid, but a legislative process in which the representatives have majority public support instead of the opposite will have an easier time tackling long-term and sensitive issues such as healthcare for a progressively expanding older population, or public sector pensions and pensions in general. There is no shortage of major political issues to address, but it never happens because the FPTP voting system makes majority government with minority support the default option. It sucks votes into a two-party system, which underpins and prolongs dictatorial decision making.

A worrying trend, designed to overcome the lack of support our electoral system confers to governments, is the recent use of Mass Formation Psychosis, or if you don't like those words, the carpet bombing of the population with relentless propaganda and the brutal censorship of dissenting voices by directing mainstream media and the huge social media companies to promote the desired responses and to shut down any opposition.

The dichotomy of our governance and the electoral process, this two-camp battle, creates an imperative to win at all costs and the money that political parties raise, with all the corruptive practices that brings about, helps distort the messaging to artificially create the differences they want the public to focus upon.

However, the problems do not end there.

Highly proportional systems and the coalitions that result create a similarly dictatorial governance, though they are usually much more strained and subject to individual and competing ideologies, which can make it even more difficult to address very contentious issues. With FPTP, most people's votes simply don't count, and this is how we confer power without support.

Typically, in a UK general election, less than 70% of the people who bothered to register to vote do so. In local elections it is around 30%; in a recent by-election it was 24%. This is quite bizarre, firstly, if one isn't bothered about voting, why register, but more importantly why would anyone forego their constitutional rights to choose their leader?

The answer to this requires a little understanding about human motivation.

We are extremely rational beings and constantly judge benefit against effort, or expenditure. We recognise value and revere that as in equal measure we understand and ignore valueless acts or objects. We do things based upon their value to us.

In order to increase voter engagement, postal voting was extended to all who wanted it, despite the increased risks of fraud. In reality it had little or no effect at all, because by making it easier the value of the act was further decreased. Achievement has value, everyone understands that the harder you work for your successes the more value they have. Ironically, to increase voter participation one needs to increase the value of voting and one way to do that is to make it harder, not easier.

Here's a way to significantly increase participation in local elections independently of the other value-diminishing effects of FPTP voting systems.

Firstly, we need a national register of voters. Currently we have this bizarre system whereby local authorities create a local register for each election. We are all familiar with the regular postal communications about who in your household is eligible to vote. It changes every election because people move, get married, and die etc., even the electoral identification number one is allocated can change each time. The simplest way to do this is to confer a right to vote to every person when they become eligible. That right then remains with the person until death. It becomes a part of who you are, and as we are a nation, it must be a national system.

In each election for which one is eligible to vote, it would be that, subject to exemptions, a registered voter will vote. If a registered voter (not exempt) decides not to vote, a default assumption would be made that they no longer wish to vote and their voter registration would then be marked as inactive, meaning they would be unable to vote again. Should they wish to restore their voting status to active, they would simply apply to do so, at a small cost of, say £25.00. The value of a vote has suddenly increased to £25.00. One doesn't need compulsion, just effective motivation. However, the apathy around voting in general has far deeper roots.

The principal factor that decreases the value of voting is the perceived effect of the act on outcome. If one lives in a constituency which is dominated by one party the value of your vote is diminished, regardless of whether you support the party that will definitely win, or some other candidate. If you do not support the party that will win your vote is completely valueless, so why bother? If you do support the party that will win, your vote won't make that win any better, nor will it confer any additional parliamentary voting power (unlike F2PTP, which will do this), hence why bother to vote?

A second, and surprising reason is the oft expressed view that politicians are all the same, only in it for themselves, nothing will change, so why bother? Is it just me or is that an extremely perceptive observation?

Imagine for a moment that you are playing a slot machine, but this one has no lights or whirring wheels, neither does it play music, it is just a box that you put a coin into. You insert a coin into this machine, and a coin comes out which is twice the value of the coin you inserted. You don't even have to press a button. This happens every time you insert a coin.

Would you continue to insert coins, or walk away?

Now imagine that when you insert your coin, the machine returns nothing at all, every time, and you knew that it would never return anything; would your behaviour change?

Quite simply, for most people, voting returns nothing to them.

The public political position toward voter engagement, that is, what the politicians say they want, is that they would like more of it and that we should encourage everyone to vote. Australia and a number of other countries have compulsory voting, which is enforced, showing yet another downside of dictatorial government and a total misunderstanding of human motivation. The real position in the UK is that politicians don't care because a win is a win, and the legitimacy of a vote because of low numbers of people participating is not considered an issue. If, in a constituency of 70,000 people, one candidate gets 100 votes and the other 99, it's still a win and considered to be entirely legitimate, despite the obvious fact that it isn't, at all, representative.

Getting a result from one's vote will encourage more people to vote.

The FPTP voting system in 2017 rendered 85% of the votes cast ineffective with respect to governance. That figure is made up of:

- Votes cast for losing candidates
- Votes cast for winning non-Conservative candidates

- Votes cast for winning Conservative candidates over and above the number of votes needed to win.

The Conservative Party only needed 5,305,259 votes to win the election and to form a government. They got more, of course, but extra votes are irrelevant.

The current voting system FPTP disenfranchises so many people that voting, particularly in constituencies where the result is a foregone conclusion, is truly an honourable but pointless discharge of duty.

The second and quite bizarre and archaic feature of our parliamentary system, is that every MP has one vote. Once elected they all have the same voting power despite their levels of support in the election.

More proportional PR systems, as we've discussed, still lead to the establishment of a parliamentary dictatorship and none of these systems (except the F2PTP solution described later) addresses parliamentary inequality.

Why should the votes of the voters in the Western Isles (Na h-Eileanan an Iar) be 5 times more valuable than the votes of the voters in Knowsley or Bristol West. Angus MacNeil was elected for the constituency of Na h-Eileanan an Iar with 6013 votes in 2017, whereas George Howarth was elected for Knowsley with 47,351. When these MPs walk into a lobby their votes count as equal.

This is utter nonsense, an inequality of breathtaking proportions. Even in this most peculiar election for UKIP in 2017, Tim Aker, a UKIP candidate, got 10,112 votes to Angus MacNeil's 6013, yet MacNeil is the MP.

Whilst this is an extreme example, a wide disparity in support is commonplace between MPs. It is simply undemocratic to halve or quarter the value of people's votes as it is to multiply the value of others. A principle of democracy is that, not only should we have an entitlement to one vote, my vote should count as equal to your vote, or anyone else's. This is not the case.

There are many other advantages to updating the voting manner and processes of the UK parliament.

Imagine how much fairer, how much more proportional it would be if MPs' votes reflected the number of votes they received in the election?

No longer will MPs have to be present to vote as they will vote using modern technology, an app, for example, whereby a minister can vote even if on a foreign trip. Currently voting is done by entering a room called a lobby. There is a Yes lobby and a No lobby. Two Tellers man each one and count the bodies in. They then report the result to the Speaker and the House.

The process, whilst understandable 300 years ago, is quaint, but archaic, time-consuming, totally dependent upon physical presence and requiring a 'buddy system' to account for absences. It is time to change. When a vote is called, it would matter not where the MP was physically located. Within an allotted period between the opening of the vote and its closing, members would cast their votes on the app, and the results would be displayed immediately. Were we to go on the 2017 election results, as above, George Howarth would vote and cast 47,351 votes, whilst Angus MacNeil would vote and cast his 6013 votes.

It would be hard to disagree that this is much fairer and a more representative method, much closer to the ideals of democracy and with many advantages.

However, not everyone thinks so.

In early 2018, I had been asked to appear on the then named *Daily Politics*. The once flagship midday BBC political program.

I was there defending the beleaguered UKIP leader Henry Bolton, then currently headline news for his personal relationship problems. Arguing against me was Peter Whittle, a former UKIP deputy leader and London Assembly member, now a successful pundit on various outlets and with his own engaging political podcast. Peter wanted Henry to step down as leader, I was arguing for him to remain. As it happened Henry subsequently lost the leadership, UKIP had committed leadership and electoral suicide and pretty well all the people who were baying for Henry's blood also left the party (including Peter Whittle) after it descended into obscurity, as I had argued it would.

Back to the story. Whilst waiting to go on, I was joined by Jacob Rees-Mogg, and spent a few minutes chatting. I talked about electoral reform and mentioned the F2PTP system. He listened and asked pertinent questions but favoured the existing FPTP voting system, which was unsurprising, and introduced a feature of the existing lobbying system in that it was one of the few times that a back bencher could buttonhole a minister. That approach not only displays a lack of imagination and openness to change but exemplifies the disdain that the ministers have for their own members, let alone their constituents. This is a system that is desperately in need of updating.

Casting our minds back to voting and the value of voting: under FPTP most votes don't count and so are perceived as having little value. Once they have been cast, they are never used again. Under my proposal (F2PTP), the vote you cast in an election is used again and again every time the MP you voted for, votes in the House of Commons. This is the 'Living Vote'.

The proposals in this book stop at the description above of how your vote is continually used in the parliamentary process, but there are some interesting options created by the Living Vote, perhaps even the retention of vote ownership for an entire parliament.

Imagine that it were possible also to rescind your vote, or even reallocate it? By way of example, were an MP to be found fiddling their expenses or behaving in an inappropriate manner, could the people who voted for them initially, subsequently choose to rescind that support? The current system allows for deselection, but this is way more fun. Anything that extends the will, and the power, of the people has to be worth considering.

Chapter Summary.

The disproportionate nature of our voting system is astonishing. Millions of people are disenfranchised, and millions of votes wasted. As a result, many simply don't bother to vote.

FPTP also aids the formation of dictatorial governments and oppositions, by sucking support into only two parties. Voting systems that are representative also tend to produce coalitions, with the objective of creating majority government, and by virtue of that, the same sort of dictatorial structure.

Under F2PTP, votes live on; and every vote cast for a candidate counts throughout the parliament.

We can do much better.

The next chapter:

Discusses some of the more familiar proportional voting systems in use and explains the deficiencies and limitations of them.

Chapter 3

Other Voting Systems

The point about fairer representation is that more people can influence the way that political power can be expressed. Many parties, including the Labour Party in 1997, wanted the electoral system changed, principally because they thought that the existing FPTP system was limiting their chances of a shot at government. Essentially, they wanted a better chance of success.

That is currently true of the Liberal Democrats, Reform UK, the Green Party and UKIP, who all believe they would benefit electorally from the change, which is true.

Despite the manifesto commitment in the Labour Party's 1997 manifesto, a resounding win, and a 178-seat majority, saw the death of that promise. Perhaps, when they've been out of power for long enough it will again become an electoral promise, but the reality is that eventually the Labour Party will win power again. Despite the fact that they are doing their level best not to win an election with a succession of poor leaders, eventually the pendulum will swing their way as it always has done. It looks as if they are happy with this state of affairs.

The Conservative Party like their odds when it comes to winning. The 13 years of New Labour was an aberration, it isn't usually that long, so when Labour wins again, it will only be for a short time and the Tories will come charging back for another 15 or 20 years, and so it continues, but it's hard to see Labour winning in 2024 as the Tories will have probably jettisoned the blond one by then, and with a bit of diligent housekeeping and a polished candidate as leader, their odds still look good. When the Conservative government is more socialist than the Labour opposition, one either goes further left, tried that, or conjures up a magical potion.

It remains, therefore, that the best chance of a referendum on voting reform rests with a disillusioned Labour Party, promising a referendum for those few extra votes. It also remains highly likely that they will win an election again, under the present system, so would be in a position to make it happen.

I'm not looking at voting reform from a party perspective, because I am no longer a member of any political party and do not intend to be one again. Neither am I interested in standing for election or otherwise benefitting from an electoral change. I think that better representation will lead to better government and a limit on governmental power will make the whole process a little more honest.

Despite the overwhelming odds against changing a system that benefits the powerful, these ideas need to be out there and part of the debate.

In this chapter I'll discuss the various alternative voting systems that have been used. Interestingly there is no consensus on which is the best one. Here is a list of some elections and the voting system used:

- European Parliament – d'Hondt System
- Welsh Assembly – Additional Member System
- Scottish Parliament – Additional Member System
- Republic of Ireland – Single Transferable Vote
- Sweden – National Proportional (4% bar)

I'll explain each of these systems and their respective problems though there are disadvantages that are common to all of them. These being:

- Every one of these systems will produce coalition governments.
- Every one of these systems tends to exclude independent candidates.

- Every one of these systems is hugely complex.
- None of these systems has the multiple advantages of the voting system and HOC structure described in this book.

There is support for a voting system which improves representation, but as I've already indicated the concept of coalition government, weakened constituency representation, and the utter complexity, makes it difficult to convince voters that it would produce better government. Unless a government were to mandate a system without a referendum, any system likely to gain voter support and win a referendum will not have the weaknesses listed above.

Assuming that any change in the voting system will need to be ratified by a national referendum, it's not just the bells and whistles that need to sparkle. If your football team has the greatest strikers and midfield players in the world but the defensive line and goalkeeper positions are filled by 70-year-old women, you'll not win many games. It's actually worse than that, because one big negative is akin to a huge hole in the bottom of the boat. When it comes to referendums one needs to avoid things the people really don't like.

As far as the detailed operation of STV, d'Hondt, Additional Member, and wholly proportional systems are concerned, there are full descriptions online as are the variations for different countries, so I will not repeat them here. I'll outline them though and then explain their deficiencies, in particular the elements of them that have the biggest negative scores.

In the UK we have this feature in our existing voting system of direct representation. We do not have a national election but 650 local ones. A vote is held in each constituency that has a number of candidates standing. The winner of a constituency election is elected to parliament with specific responsibility for the constituency they stood in. Once elected they represent everyone, they press for the well-being of their constituency and their constituents and make themselves available to help constituents with all sorts of problems. Hence you will often hear phrases such as 'my constituents' and 'in my constituency', etc. Also, it is not uncommon for MPs to present themselves as having been personally elected, with terms such as 'I have been returned with an increased majority' and the like.

With each MP firmly tied to a geographical area the connection between one person and about 120,000 people (72,000 voters) is about as strong as it can be. You may think that it isn't all that strong when looking at this numerical relationship, and you would be right, but as far as one can tell the British people really like this connection. The sense that an ordinary person can see, talk to and email a member of the legislature, a VIP in most people's minds, is a benefit not replicated everywhere. For example, in Sweden, where I spend quite a bit of time, the notion that one has direct access to a parliamentarian is viewed with astonishment. In this bastion of Nordic proportionality politicians are as elite and detached as it is possible to be.

The last two paragraphs represent the most generous interpretation of the local role of a constituency MP. In reality, most of it simply isn't true.

MPs do not represent everyone in a constituency, they firstly represent their party and will vote how they are told, regardless of the effect on any individual. Occasionally, they will take up a local cause, but it helps if there is also a photo opportunity and a bit of positive fluff in the local media. The 'constituency' work, that most MPs like to emphasise, doesn't stretch too far with a 1 to 120,000 relationship, but they do spend time cultivating their constituency associations, garden parties etc. After all, these are the people who tread the streets for them, donate cash and man the stalls.

Despite the limitations, the practice, and the practicalities of the constituency link, it remains fundamental. It is a good thing, and it is better than not having that. Any voting system that totally precluded that, such as a national proportional system, or watered it down to nothing, like the Party List system (d'Hondt an example) or even STV or AM, is likely to get the thumbs down from the voters.

However, increased proportionality always means bigger constituencies, therefore a diluting of responsibility to some degree. The F2PTP part of F2PTP-IND only requires the doubling of constituency sizes, and because of its unique feature of electing two people from opposite sides of the political spectrum, is most likely to give people a representative who is more in line with their own views. The Independents will have much larger constituencies but will also provide an ear not beholden to any party ideology.

STV constituencies will be four or more times the size of the present constituency. Assuming an STV constituency of six, there would be six potential contacts for an individual. That might seem good but the opportunity to weasel out of those inconvenient roles is also massively increased.

STV.

The Single Transferable Vote. This system presents the voter with one ballot paper with multiple candidates on it. The voter's task is to mark against, not just one name, but also make a second choice. They may be asked to rank down to the number of seats available, so in a six-candidate constituency you may be required to rank your choices in order, one to six.

When the votes are counted the total number of votes is known. In this example let's say 300,000 people voted, there are six seats, therefore any candidate whose vote total is greater than 50,000 is elected. This is called the quota. Let's say that candidate A received 70,001 votes, 50,001 secured the seat, so 20,000 are reallocated to the second choice on 20,000 ballot papers. But, which 20,000? One lot of 20,000 ballot papers may have quite different second choices to another lot of 20,000. The answer is to move a proportion of everyone's vote, that is

20,000/70,000 = 0.285714 of everyone's vote goes the way of the second choice. Candidates with the lowest votes are eliminated and all of their votes also going to second choices.

Confused yet? And we're only halfway there. Of course, a computer is needed to work out the eventual result, and it does produce a result. In my view, this particular team not only has elderly ladies on the back row, but also in midfield (apologies to elderly ladies).

Geeks love this system, and most proponents of fairer voting are wedded to it. Make Votes Matter declare no interest, but if we get PR without a referendum, it will be this system.

Some of the specific downsides are:

- The constituency link is severely weakened.
- There will be a lot of names on the ballot paper. Upwards of 35 or 40.
- Donkey voting.
  - All list systems are subject to this phenomenon. When faced with a long list people tend to start at the top with 1 and work down. Imagine, for example, that you are a Labour supporter and there are 6 Labour candidates on the ballot paper. Naturally, you want Labour to win, so you mark the first Labour name with your first choice, the second Labour candidate as your second choice etc. It's pure luck as to where each person comes on the list as ballot papers are in alphabetical order of the candidates' surnames. The Labour candidate who is highest on the list will get the lion's share of first choice votes. This does not encourage people to be cognitively selective when voting and the number of votes the candidates get isn't a true reflection of real choice but convenience which is driven by this complicated system.

- You vote for a person, then they take your vote away from them and give it to someone else without your knowledge.
- The system treats your second choice with the same value as your first, yet it must be subordinate, because it is a second choice. This is clearly illogical.
- Some people get to vote twice and others three times and others just once. This undermines the principle of one person one vote.
- It relies on people making second and third choices. This is an inherent flaw because if nobody makes a second choice the system fails. That means even if insufficient people make second choices it fails.
- Computer generated results are at risk of being manipulated by hacking much more easily than hand-counted votes.
- Filling mid-term vacancies is a real problem.
- The killer, and though I've mentioned it before, it deserves to be repeated, this system will lead to grubby coalitions.

As I mentioned before there are real weaknesses with this system that can easily be exploited in a campaign. As the AV system of the 2011 referendum was holed beneath the waterline by major deficiencies, so would be STV.

Additional Member System.

AM is a hybrid system with constituency voting and regional voting. AM uses FPTP, the existing system for UK Parliamentary elections for a proportion of the seats vacant, and a party list system on a regional basis for the remainder.

Scotland uses a version of this system for the Scottish Parliament Elections; many think that it was specifically chosen to ensure that the SNP could never have an overall majority, though that didn't really work. Of the 129 MSPs in the Scottish Parliament 73 are chosen using FPTP and 56 from the party list system. Like FPTP, independent candidates stand little chance of being elected and no chance on a party list system as it is for parties only. It is designed to minimise the unfairness of FPTP, yet still retains that aspect for most of the seats.

A major problem for the AM system is that it keeps FPTP for the majority of the seats and is highly likely to create coalition government with not more or less equal partners but with a massive majority partner and a very small party. As we see elsewhere, these arrangements give minorities far more power and influence than their electoral support warrants.

The regional aspect of AM is an add-on. It is a way to mitigate the effects of FPTP and offers nothing more than the illusion of greater representation when the opposite is true.

Oddly the devolution arrangements for Scotland added 129 more politicians, a brand-new parliament and civil service, but with no reduction in the number of Westminster MPs, which remained at 59.

Apart from the fact that Scottish voters are massively over-represented in the UK parliament, an annoying anomaly was created. I say annoying, because as previously explained they have no power because the government of the day, whether created by a party majority or by a coalition, acts as a dictatorship. Scottish MPs have been known to vote one way on an issue in Scotland and the opposite way for England. They also have a disproportionately large say over English only matters, subject to the law of irrelevance above, whilst English MPs have no say in Scottish laws that are within the devolutionary powers.

The AM system is also used to populate the Welsh Assembly. It is less convoluted than STV, but like all PR systems, other than a national proportional system, doesn't address the disregard of support in Parliament where every member's vote carries equal weight regardless of how many people voted for them.

The politician's argument for the equality of membership, is that Parliament is a level playing field and to perform their tasks honourably and successfully they must all have equal standing. It is a parliamentary tradition which has worked well, and to make the changes I am suggesting would create second- and third-class MPs, which would be to the detriment of the parliamentary process.

In reality, this is an illusion and, as is usual in these matters, is all about the politicians whilst disregarding the voters. Because of our voting system the source of power, which should rest with the voter, is diluted again and again in order to create something which is convenient for politicians and is a disadvantage of all voting systems, including those that purport to be proportional, with the exception of a national list system.

D'Hondt and party list systems.

Party list systems of which the d'Hondt is one, are based on national or regional geographical areas. The ballot paper contains all the parties contesting the election, though once again there is no place for independent candidates. The population of each geographical area votes and parliamentary seats are awarded, based on how many votes each party won. The calculations may vary a bit as do the areas, but it is simple and is used in many European countries and for European Parliament elections.

If the party list is national it has the greatest proportionality; if it is regional as the former UK European Parliament elections were, the proportionality is reduced. However, if proportionality is the main concern, then this achieves that as well as any other system.

For the UK though, there are two major drawbacks. Firstly, the connection we have, and which is well regarded by the British people, of the strong link between a representative and a geographical area is lost. The concept of contacting your MP to discuss a personal issue doesn't exist, and as I've already said, any mention of that to a Swede, elicits looks of confusion and astonishment.

Secondly, the coalitions needed to form a government tend to involve many parties, even the very small ones, which has the effect of distorting the power balance with ministerial appointments and undue influence driven by party dogma. Imagine, for example, that were the Labour Party, the SNP and the Greens to form a coalition, with the Greens' single seat being the deciding factor as to whether the government can pass legislation or not, this would elevate the power of the Green MP to a point far beyond their party support.

Opposition parties will mostly vote against, because the act of a government failing to get a vote through often results in a vote of no confidence in the government. This leads to a fuelling of extreme motivation for the government to succeed and for the opposition to scupper that intended success.

Like most voting systems there are variations of them everywhere, but none achieves a parliamentary state of government without coalition and total dominance except the mechanisms described in this book.

A parliament is there to represent and enact the people's will as best it can. All of these alternative systems work, in the sense that they produce choices through the process. What this book describes is a way to better underpin the choice of representative, by bringing more people into the process, significantly increasing representation, and as a result, get better government. It is a unique and novel idea.

Interestingly these alternative systems we've just discussed are the very opposite of new.

The Single Transferable Vote was developed by Thomas Wright Hill in 1819, d'Hondt system by Victor d'Hondt in 1882, the Additional Member System, sometime after 1944 by the Hansard Society. A lot has changed since 1819, so perhaps it is now time for a fresh look at the balance of power in Parliament and how we determine who should wield it?

Chapter Summary.

All the alternative systems lead to coalition governments. As it is likely that any change will be subject to a referendum according to precedent, this is a major weakness. Other things people don't like is unfathomable complexity.

The next chapter:

Looks at where we are now with regard to achieving reform.

Chapter 4

Where are we Now?

Disappointingly, I think the short answer to the question this chapter asks is still in the same place.

The Conservative Party is in government at the moment and likely to be for a while, and they will never change a voting system that is so beneficial to them in winning elections. The Labour Party in the past have included a firm commitment to voting reform in their 1997 manifesto but ditched it when they received a huge majority. That commitment then vanished in the subsequent Labour election victories. The Labour Party will be in government again eventually, but even if the next one also commits to voting reform, there is no guarantee that it will be enacted, and if it were, the incentive for them to choose a system that would benefit them is probable.

One of the problems, one of the ones my proposals will fix, is the duality of our electoral system and the oscillating nature of it. Oddly, this arrangement suits both major parties rather well, because it excludes anyone else, which is good (for them) and pretty much guarantees that Labour will be in power for around a third of the time with the Tories taking two-thirds. Even with the lurch to the left under the Corbyn leadership and his deficiencies as a leader, millions of people still voted Labour.

2017

The Conservatives polled 13,636,684 votes and gained total power with DUP help.

Labour polled 12,877,918 votes with zero power.

2019

The Conservatives polled 13,966,454 votes and gained total power.

Labour polled 10,269,051 votes with zero power.

Despite the resultant effect of the FPTP voting system in terms of the exercise of power, support remained pretty high for a party with so many leadership deficiencies. In 2019, both parties were aided by The Brexit Party, standing down candidates which mainly benefitted the Conservative Party. The 2019 election was a Brexit election. As the figures show, the principal factor was a collapse of the Labour vote, and a much smaller increase in the Conservative one.

One has to assume, therefore, that when the Labour Party has an acceptable leader and has moved once again toward the centre, they will win. It might take a couple of further losses to cement their faith in voting reform, even though all current incarnations of voting reform result with the same problems we have now, which is the concentration of power in one person.

There are some Labour MPs and some Conservative MPs, who support, or say they support voting reform. There are a number of organisations that have campaigned for years to bring such change about, but in reality, we are where we have always been. Nowhere. We, and I mean all those who support voting reform, are no further forward in this quest and there are some reasons for that.

It's not easy to draw people together on this, which is why, for example, we have multiple organisations supportive of electoral reform, and multiple parties. For the latter the practicalities of our voting system dictate that there should be only one. Splitting the vote under FPTP achieves nothing. Different organisations form different views and unsurprisingly are reluctant to change their position. The phenomenon is often referred to as the 'not invented here syndrome', and effectively blocks any progress.

In 2017 I held the portfolio for electoral reform when Henry Bolton won the leadership of UKIP. I devised a strategy to coalesce support and I wrote about it at the time to move the project forward.

The principal elements of my article were:

By proportionality, I mean the voting power in the House of Commons that each MP is authorised to wield. A PR system is designed to be proportional (as much as could possibly be the case) to the numbers of people that voted for each MP. However, the activity I describe as 'voting power' in most descriptions of PR is often commonly analogous to and understood to mean seats. This is, in fact, not necessarily the case as voting power is the real issue here and it is not necessarily synonymous with seats. In fact, in some PR scenarios, they are quite different.

Proportional Representation is a term that is commonly used to describe proportional voting systems that improve the proportionality between 'voting power' and electoral support.

As the UKIP cabinet member for Electoral Reform, I intend to drive the agenda with new and different arguments, a structured strategy, and a perspective on the subject to stimulate interest and thinking on what would be the most significant constitutional change since the establishment of parliament – yes, even bigger than Brexit.

Opportunities have come and gone, though a further one will appear. It is for this future opportunity that I accepted this position, and it is toward this that I shall work. This time though the lessons of the past will be heeded, and the same mistakes will not be made again.

To be successful we need the following:

1. *The right arguments.*
2. *The full support of the party.*
3. *The support and cooperation of like-minded organisations and political parties.*
4. *A mechanism to choose which electoral system suits the UK best.*

> 5. *A channel through which we can direct the voting intentions of those who are drawn to our cause, away from parties that wish to preserve their self-interest and toward parties that support this change.*
>
> *The present situation is characterised by disparate organisations with different ideas as to how electoral reform is going to be achieved and different ideas as to which 'off the shelf' system would be best, with some preferring to leave that hoary old chestnut to the end. Just coordinating the effort and goodwill of all these groups can raise the profile in the minds of the public.*

Whilst cooperation in politics is often the best way to get results it isn't always possible. I reached out to all the organisations and parties proposing a working together and a structures approach but with little effect.

UKIP at that time was still a major political party and you might have thought that an approach from a national spokesperson would have warranted at least an acknowledgement. Although the 2017 vote was diminished significantly from the heady 3.8 million in 2015, UKIP still got more votes than the Green Party (Green 525,665, UKIP 594,068) and its alter ego The Brexit Party, which dominated the last EU elections in 2019.

Clearly, our political parties and quasi-political organisations will not cooperate on an issue they agree upon if they disagree with some other political ideology of a proposed partner. As of writing there is a very similar situation in Sweden, where electoral representatives of one party refuse to work with political representatives of another party. The electorate, it seems, don't count.

Since 2017 nothing has moved forward with respect to voting or electoral reform. Activity appears to be the objective, not results. As the grandly sounding Electoral Reform Society was founded in 1884 and we still have the FPTP system in 2022, perhaps we shouldn't hold our collective breath.

One could claim that some movement has taken place but that's only for recent elections, new political bodies like the Scottish Parliament, Welsh Assembly, London Assembly, and the former EU elections when we were still members, but the important stuff hasn't changed. In reality, all the elections that don't count have been allowed to be proportional. However, even in these quasi-proportional elections exactly the same thing results. Instead of outright majority that FPTP tend to produce, we have a majority built from coalition. Small parties with little electoral support get to wield excess influence, which detracts somewhat from the restraining nature of one's coalition partners.

From a governance perspective, all the real power is in parliament and local authorities. Both these elections are held under FPTP.

My own view is that the most probable way forward for a more proportional voting system is through the Labour Party when they next win an election. This is more likely to happen if they also lose the next one and perhaps the one after, because they'll definitely be getting desperate. Sir Keir Starmer may well have stood down by then and perhaps a clear-out of the hard left will have been completed. As soon as they become electable again with a charismatic leader untainted by allegations of inaction in a former role and a more moderate face of the party as a whole, they'll get their turn.

The other option would be the Brexit strategy, which I'll discuss in a later paragraph.

Chapter Summary.

It doesn't look as if much has changed. It also doesn't look as if much will change.

The next chapter:

Describes the voting system F2PTP and its benefits.

Chapter 5

First Two Past the Post (F2PTP), How it Works and the Benefits

F2PTP is a voting system designed for UK parliamentary elections. It works in exactly the same way as the current system as far as the voter is concerned. A ballot paper is produced with the names of the candidates and their party in exactly the same way as we are used to. As a voter you will mark a cross against your preferred choice, as now. The ballot papers are collected and counted as now.

This chapter describes the voting system and the effects of the changes on the levels of representation. However, it is only a part of the total solution. The role of independent candidates completes the new election concept and is described in the next chapter, but the election of party candidates and independent candidates both use the F2PTP voting rules.

What Changes?

The first difference is that the first placed and second placed candidates will be elected, whereas only the winner is elected under the current system.

The second difference is that the constituency size will be approximately twice the size of your current constituency.

In all other aspects, the election under F2PTP will be identical to former elections under FPTP, the current system. This makes it simple to understand because it's something we've been used to for a long time. Despite the fact that the constituency sizes are bigger, each party can only enter one candidate, as is the case now.

Nothing much changes from the voting angle, but the interpretation of the results and their application changes everything.

In a Nutshell.

F2PTP is a voting system where the first and second placed candidates are elected.

When voting in Parliament each elected member casts the same number of votes as they received in the election.

The F2PTP paper

The F2PTP system was developed in 2015 and the results of the 2010 and 2015 general elections overlayed onto the system to produce a set of results that would have occurred had the F2PTP system actually been used. In reality, of course, when people voted, second place wasn't an elected position, so their normal voting behaviour was exhibited. In a changed environment under F2PTP where second place returned an elected position, voting behaviour would most certainly have changed and the improved representation shown in the F2PTP paper would most likely be even better than the exercise shows.

The full paper, with the electoral number, tables and the justifications for the improvements in representation detailed below, is included as Appendix 1.

The first problem was to create the larger constituencies. With two MPs being elected for each parliamentary constituency there would have to be roughly half the number of them, or we would simply double the number of MPs, which is far from desirable. Because of national boundaries the final number is slightly less than the expected 325.

The easiest way to do this was to combine existing constituencies, so I set about this with electoral maps and manually created the combinations of constituencies needed for the exercise. Once I had the constituencies the numbers of votes actually cast in the election were summed, the first and second placed candidates of the new larger constituency revealed and the necessary calculations undertaken.

I then compared the factual election results with the alternative election results to see what had changed and what the effect of those changes were on overall representation.

The advantages of F2PTP as a voting system alone are as follows:

Simplicity of operation.

Nothing really changes from the voting mechanism we are used to. People receive a ballot paper and choose which candidate to vote for. The procedure is the same as we are used to: choose the candidate you want. The result of the election is measured in exactly the same way as now, your votes are added up. The winner and second place candidates are declared elected. There is no switching of votes, no second choices, no artificial manipulation as with other PR systems. It is totally transparent.

Increased representation.

Under F2PTP, around one and a half times more people get the candidate they voted for. This is a hugely significant improvement, which is likely to be even greater when people know, before casting their vote, that second places are also elected. As we know the FPTP system deters people from voting in accordance with their preferred choices because the tactical aspect in a two-party state is huge. Knowing that your preferred candidate cannot win in your constituency, there is an incentive to either choose the lesser of two evils or decline to vote. Result declarations are the same as now, equally quickly determined as now, because the process is the same as now.

No wasted votes.

In 2010, around five and a half million votes were wasted, and in 2015 around seven and a half million. Under F2PTP these numbers would be zero. A wasted vote is one cast in excess of the number of votes needed to elect the winner of an FPTP constituency contest and is often referred to as a majority. For example, if the winner of a constituency election received 30,000 votes and the second placed candidate only 15,000 votes, the difference is referred to as the elected person's majority and is often used to suggest the relative safety of the parliamentary seat. Other than the inference that the bigger the majority the more difficult it would be to overturn the result and for the holder of a 15,000 majority to lose their seat, it is a completely worthless measure.

In 2010, just over fifteen and a half million people voted for losing candidates, an ineffective vote, but certainly not wasted as the candidates that lost needed every vote they got, and more. In 2015 this number was just under fifteen and a half million votes. Under F2PTP, these numbers would have been nine million and eight million respectively. Between six and seven million more people would have got the person they voted for.

It cannot be emphasised enough that this would have caused such a dramatic improvement in voter representation, even when people had no idea that second place would count. Imagine what might happen when they do know?

The 'living vote'.

The principle of parliamentary representation is based on one person one vote, but it doesn't end up like that. Once a representative is elected, they have one vote in the chamber, regardless of how many people cast their votes for them in the election. The most extreme example in most previous elections is the one previously cited for the 2017 election results earlier:

George Howarth received 47,351 votes, whilst Angus MacNeil got 6013 votes, but in Parliament they have one vote each. The votes of the voters in the Western Isles effectively have almost eight times the value of the votes of each voter in Knowsley. That's hardly upholding the one person one vote principle. Whilst this is the most extreme example of the difference between votes cast and parliamentary power exercised, such differences are extensive, and many wide disparities exist. This is not an isolated case.

Whilst one can understand how such a system grew, it is no longer appropriate because we can easily use technology to do the awkward counting, to simplify and make more convenient the voting mechanisms in Parliament.

This aspect of the F2PTP system has more of an attraction than just repairing the equilibrium between voters and their representatives' power. Apart from the unfairness of having your vote discarded, unwanted and unused, even when the person you voted for was elected, the current system removes the voter from the equation. Your vote was cast, the votes counted, the result declared, and all votes then forgotten. With the F2PTP voting system, your vote lives on throughout the representative's tenure and would be repeatedly cast every time they vote.

Votes per seat become more equal.

Votes per seat is a broad measure to show the disparity in fairness. For example, the Conservative and Labour parties, over the two elections reconstituted under the F2PTP system, typically needed between 30,000 and 40,000 votes per seat. Other parties fare much worse. In 2010 the Liberal Democrats and Others needed around 120,000 votes per seat; in 2015, UKIP's figure was 3,876,674 votes per seat; and the Greens' 1,155,375 votes per seat. Under F2PTP, these figures were much more even. In 2010, the Conservative Party, Labour

Party and Liberal Democrats all had between 40,000 and 50,000 votes per seat with others at 98,000. In 2015 the lowest was 26,323 and the highest of the known parties 86,148, with only others over 200,000 and just 1 seat. The general spread was much more closely aligned.

It would be true to say that F2PTP over FPTP dramatically equalises the votes per seat needed. This represents an automatic improvement in representation.

The 'opposites' effect. Strengthening constituency representation.

F2PTP is truly a unique voting system with many benefits, but one is extraordinarily interesting and can only serve to improve the political landscape. This system removes stark geographical political division. The north/south divide, as well as Red Wall and Blue Wall seats simply disappear. This alone would be a powerful reason to change, even if all the other benefits didn't exist.

Each constituency elects the first placed and second placed candidates. The rules of the system prohibit parties from entering two candidates for the two vacant electoral positions, but such a rule wouldn't be necessary in reality. It simply doesn't make sense for a party to do this because they will split their own vote and probably not make first or second place.

In an election the second-place candidate would typically hold a different political ideology to the winner. In most constituencies it would be either Conservative first, and Labour second, or the other way round. Red Walls and Blue Walls simply disappear because each constituency would have one Conservative and one Labour MP. Constituents in these larger constituencies would have representatives each with an opposing political ideology which would vary depending upon the constituency. Labour Party supporting constituents, or Liberal Democrats, have a better chance of raising issues with people who hold similar political views. Whole swathes of the country would have representation from a different perspective, in essence, a different kind of broader representation which is not provided by any other voting system.

No sectarian enclaves.

The most obvious one is in Scotland with the SNP. Despite the fact that this party enjoys total political domination with a minority of the popular vote in the Scottish Parliament elections, the process borders on the absurd in a UK general election, where a miserable 3.9% of the vote affords them 48 seats in the UK Parliament. An odd outcome for a disastrous experiment in devolution, the most significant of which being just more politicians. This new system would end that bizarre disparity.

The British system, the FPTP system, employs the 'two wrongs make a right' principle to nullify this seemingly excess presence in Parliament. The disproportional representation of the SNP in the UK parliament is countered effectively by the dictatorial outcome of our elections and the way majority government works. In reality the 48 seats of the SNP are as ineffective as the 203 Labour seats and the 11 Liberal Democrat seats, won in the 2019 election. Even added together they are totally impotent, because as has already been explained, a majority creates an effective dictatorship and nobody else has any power at all.

Tactical voting virtually eliminated.

Tactical voting against.

The term tactical voting refers to two mechanisms. The first is the, probably widespread, tendency to vote against a party as opposed to voting for a party. This was very apparent in 2017 when I stood for UKIP in the Rochester and Strood constituency. I had a background in the constituency having worked there for many years and decided to stand there, even though I lived in an adjacent constituency.

The recent history of Rochester and Strood gave cause for some optimism, because in 2014 the then Conservative MP, Mark Reckless, joined UKIP. In an act truly supportive of democracy and, in my memory, only ever replicated by another Conservative MP Douglas Carswell. He resigned his seat, and a by-election was called, which he won narrowly. It really is taking a risk to resign a safe Conservative seat, join a much smaller and electorally unsuccessful party (in UK parliamentary elections). The single mission, which UKIP was created to achieve, couldn't create enough support to break through the FPTP barrier which is extraordinarily high, and that's a party that got over five and a half million votes in the European elections.

The fact that UKIP had previously won this seat gave some hope, however, it was scuppered by tactical voting and an increased Conservative vote.

Many people I spoke to apologised, reassuring me that they had voted UKIP before and would do so again in the future, but on this occasion, they just had to keep Corbyn out. The then Prime Minister, Theresa May, had also promised as vehemently as it was possible to do, to get Brexit done. In that election the Corbyn factor was huge, and he more than adequately filled the role of ogre.

Tactical voting, easing the path.
The other more recent gerrymandering strategy to alter election outcomes is a rather regular attempt by the Greens and the Lib Dems not to compete against each other. The idea being is that if the Lib Dems stood down then Lib Dem

voters would vote Green instead, and vice versa. I've never seen that work, by the way.

However, in the 2019 election this tactic, exercised on a much bigger scale, saw Nigel Farage stand down every Brexit Party candidate who would have stood against a Brexit supporting Conservative Party candidate. Brexit Party supporters, of whom there were in excess of five million, were asked instead to support Boris Johnson, who had supported Brexit through the referendum campaign, had been a significant influence in the referendum result and who had also promised faithfully to get Brexit done. There can be little doubt that this act of sabotage against one's own party for a greater good was instrumental in the Conservatives getting the size of majority they did.

Of course, no Brexit Party future parliamentarians were to be lost because it would have been unlikely in the extreme for any of them to have actually won a seat. However, votes for The Brexit Party take votes from Conservative and Labour, and on the Brexit issue the Labour Party still supported remaining in the European Union. It is reasonable to assume that those who would have normally supported Labour would have supported The Brexit Party. However, having a Brexit-supporting Conservative candidate and no Brexit party candidate to vote for, their votes would have, and did go to the Conservative Party. Most votes that would have been lost had a Brexit Party candidate been standing, would have been Conservative ones. It is also quite possible that people would have tactically voted for the Conservatives, as they did in the 2017 election, regardless of whether a Brexit Party candidate was standing. Nigel Farage is a very astute politician and I doubt that these possible outcomes would have escaped him.

The point is though – do either of these tactical voting mechanisms actually work under F2PTP? The answer is not really, as any outcome is much less predictable, and votes are more likely to go the way of your first preference because their electoral chances are improved by F2PTP.

Having two winners creates another problem for the potential tactical voter. If, from the candidates on the ballot paper, two will be elected, who do you vote against? If second place also counts, maybe the smaller party you support might make that lower bar, so why put your vote elsewhere? In a usual FPTP election, it's often a foregone conclusion which two parties will be first and second, and smaller parties have no chance. Smaller parties standing down to aid other smaller parties makes sense in that scenario even though they achieve nothing. However, in F2PTP, second place is much more achievable and standing down might just be throwing away an opportunity. Those who would have voted Conservative or Labour, might well go for who they really want instead of the least-worst option. When opportunities open up to get elected, voter behaviour changes.

The more representative elections are the less effect tactical voting has.

The height of the bar?

In FPTP elections the bar is set very high to win a seat. It depends also where the election is held, but for English parties, not nationalistic parties like the SNP or Plaid Cymru, polling millions of votes gets no reward. The FPTP system sucks support toward the bilateral status quo. No other party has a chance of governing, therefore only a vote for one of the two that do is worthwhile.

Fully proportional elections as in Israel or Sweden create an additional set of problems though. In Sweden the bar is set at 4% of the vote. Ironically that system in the UK would see the SNP banished from parliament. That results in a multiparty parliament with no single party having a majority, therefore having to arrange coalitions with several partners to reach the dictatorial levels needed to pass legislation.

This, however, comes at a cost. The tiny party needed to form a majority government find themselves in a position of power which far exceeds their support, and from which results ministerial positions, and policy directions that the majority of Swedish citizens do not support. Currently they're not wild about the doubling of fuel and energy prices, but it's hard to see how anything can change that much when governing entails so much compromise.

These nationally proportional systems do not embody the constituency relationship that we value so much and the concept of an independent is ruled out.

All PR systems, good and bad, complicated or simple, lead to coalitions between people who do not agree, though the dictatorial tendencies of a government are muted by such internal opposition and compromise, policies can also be enacted that nobody really wants.

Constituency boundaries become much less significant.

The drawing of constituency boundaries is a complicated task. It needn't be so, but the requirement that they should all be more or less the same size creates havoc. We have constituencies inside other constituencies and constituency boundaries crossing the middle of roads. Typically, Parliamentary boundaries do not match the local authority boundaries, let alone make use of other natural boundaries such as rivers.

F2PTP eliminates the need for constituencies to be the same size. As parliamentarians vote with the number of votes that were cast for them, a larger constituency, with a larger winners and seconds vote, will have that directly represented in the voting power of their representatives. Huge disparities in size aren't ideal, but with the greater flexibility that F2PTP affords, this wouldn't happen, except in the national regions.

The new constituency structure and the new boundaries under F2PTP create an opportunity to align parliamentary constituencies with those of local authorities and other statutory bodies. We would have the opportunity to create simplified and more aligned governmental structures and at the same time improve representation all round.

The F2PTP paper is in Appendix 1. It is a description of F2PTP only as applied to the 2010 and 2015 general elections in the UK.

Chapter Summary and Key Takeaways.

F2PTP not only increases representation, it corrects the imbalance of Parliamentary voting as well. From this apparently minor change so many other benefits are realised, such as better constituency boundaries, the Living Vote and the collapse of North/South and Red Wall/Blue Wall divides.

The next chapter:

The next chapter introduces F2PTP-IND, which combines this voting system with a new balance of power in parliament. Majority government without an overall majority. The best of both worlds.

Chapter 6

F2PTP-IND, A Total Solution

The Case for the Independent.

Incorruptibility.

In the context of the F2PTP-IND system the term 'Independent' refers to an elected member of parliament that owes no allegiance to a political party. The rules in this system of independents would also prohibit them from receiving patronage or from accepting money, gifts, promises of jobs, etc. from external agencies. They would serve limited terms, may not accept any office of state or otherwise be vulnerable to the influences that party MPs are.

The intention is to create a force in our parliament that would be immune from corruptible influences and make judgements solely based upon the arguments presented, their own personal views, education, knowledge, and political beliefs.

Knowledge of the person.

We do not vote for people in general elections. The candidate's name is on the ballot paper, but the deciding factor is the party they represent. Often, people have little idea of that person's ability, honesty, achievements, or anything else. We trust that the person is of the necessary standing in all things because they have been selected by a political party and if that party is Labour or Conservative, Liberal Democrat or Green, those assumptions are automatically acknowledged. Even the smaller parties benefit from these sometimes unwarranted assumptions. The fact that a candidate is standing for a party approved by the Electoral Commission acts as a free pass against questions of suitability.

For the independents in an F2PTP-IND election though, voters will have the opportunity to know much more about the person and they don't have to take it as read. The processes described below will subject the independent candidates to a rigorous examination of their abilities, qualifications, life achievements and personal beliefs. Something the electorate assume is entirely satisfactory for party candidates.

With the independent candidate in an F2PTP-IND general election, the voter will know much more about a person who is much less likely to be compromised by corruptible influences when in office. That's about as good as it can get.

It works like this.

- Governments would almost certainly rule as an overall minority. The party with the most Living Votes (cumulative) would form the government in all cases.
- Parliament would consist of two groups.
- Members elected on behalf of parties.
- Independent representatives with no affiliations, connections, or other associations with parties.
- Members, both the party member and the independent member, would be elected under F2PTP rules.
- In order to pass legislation, the government would need to convince a proportion of the independent members to back it. If they can't, it's probably poor law.

When the dictatorial nature of government is removed, and legislation has to elicit the support of independent members through cogent argument instead of the usual bullying, it is likely to be better thought through and better drafted.

Such a mechanism also gives parliamentary opposition real power, for they too have the option of convincing the independents to support their view, which in turn will reduce points-scoring opposition in favour of persuasion by strength of argument.

Better government would ensue were that to be broadened. A minority government is the solution, seeking support from independent members to pass legislation, thereby disincentivising the automatic opposition from other parties as well as to negate the effectiveness of the corrupt practices already mentioned.

In order to get elected in UK general elections, standing for a party is really the only way, for the independent candidate it is an impossible task. In local elections, independent candidates, and independent groups, such as Swale Independents, have seen electoral success recently, because they act as an alternative to parties which the electors no longer wish to support and the automatic perception of greater integrity that goes well with the concept of independence.

People like the concept of independence and that does transfer to independent political candidates also. However, it cannot be enacted in a general election, because of the enormous power and influence of political parties and to overcome the height of the bar.

However, in my view, independent MPs would provide a balance to our democratic process and be largely immune from the pressure to conform to party will. Parties are influenced by external factors, largely money, they impose their view on their own members with 'Whipping', a parliamentary term referring to the formal process of a party's police force making sure their members vote the right way.

The following is an example of how the distribution of seats for party MPs and independent MPs could be organised under the F2PTP-IND voting system. It is an example only, to show how voting would return members and how each member's voting power in the commons would be calculated. The only criteria to be maintained is that a quarter of MPs should be independent, or as close to that proportion as possible, and that Independent MPs' constituencies will consist of a whole number of party constituencies, depending upon the fit. In each election the voter will have two ballot papers, one with party candidates and one with independent candidates. Each voter will cast one vote on each ballot paper.

In this example I use a parliament of 640 MPs. That number is a little less than the current 650, though many are of the opinion that it should be even fewer. 512 of these seats will be contested as they are now, by political party candidates under the F2PTP voting system. 128 of the seats will be contested by independent candidates also elected under the F2PTP voting system. There will be 256 Party constituencies covering the entire UK and 64 Independent constituencies. Each of the independent constituencies will cover a number of the Parliamentary constituencies. The specific number would depend upon the fit of constituencies with administrative and county boundaries. Because under the F2PTP voting system constituency sizes are less significant, there is much more flexibility in determining constituency boundaries.

The number of 128 has been determined by the simple rationale that if one party achieves the minimum majority of 260, they would then need 50% of the independent vote to carry a motion. If the majority is higher, then fewer independent votes are needed; if the largest party is in a minority within the party seats, then a larger proportion of independent votes would be required. Basically, the number of 128 has been chosen because there has to be enough independent MPs to make a difference in passing or rejecting legislation. The proportion of approximately 25% of the legislature allows all options to be practical and achievable. Despite the fact that under F2PTP voting power of individual MPs will depend proportionally on their personal electoral support, this level of independence, broadly in the middle, is as good a way of determining something so new which has no alternative or proven method for doing so.

The true number of party constituencies and independent constituencies would depend upon the natural geographic and administrative geography as well as any intention to streamline the House of Commons by reducing the number of MPs. It's worth pointing out that the political class will be totally opposed to this system because of self-interest. Many of them will lose their privileged positions. However, we don't need to convince the elites, just the people.

The system will return party MPs and Independent MPs. The party MPs will likely be made up of the parties that currently field candidates, and as happens now, the majority of the votes would be cast for the Conservative or Labour parties, one of which would be the largest party, and entitled to form a government. The winning party will have an overall majority of the 'Living Votes' of all the party MPs, but it is unlikely to have a 'Living Vote' majority of all the MPs because a quarter of them would be independent. In this system it is not the absolute number of MPs that is important but the number of 'Living Votes' they are authorised to cast.

The government will act and draft legislation as it does now. Whether or not the governing party has a majority of the party based 'Living Votes' is much less material than now because in all cases, to pass legislation they will need to persuade a proportion of the independent MPs to vote with them. Equally, if the official opposition have a powerful argument, they too can persuade the independents to back them. This creates a fairer and better legislature, because it empowers opposition and gives them real influence through argument and not political dogma or perceived electoral advantage. By enabling government which consists of no overall majority yet can pass legislation without opportune and overtly politically motivated but inept opposition, the balance of power will be shifted away from the dictatorial structure we have now, to a body of independent representatives who will judge the legislation of the government from a position of statutorily independent authority. It is my strong view that this will create true democracy, true opposition, and better government.

Changing the make-up of Parliament and our voting systems is all about better government, which I believe will be better when there is meaningful opposition. Government is better when it isn't all-powerful, and it is better when it has to convince those who support its agenda by argument, as opposed to coercion.

Better representation means a more representative parliament. In a parliament elected with a more representative voting system and the introduction of independents who hold the balance of power, Governments can still rule, but not dominate. If government is better, that means better legislation and better outcomes. It really is time for change.

The F2PTP system is a voting system, and Appendix 1 shows the application of this methodology as applied to the 2010 and 2015 general elections. In other words, a perspective of what would have happened if the votes cast were distributed using the F2PTP methodology. The theoretical results, of course, don't represent entirely what would have happened had people known that second place counted. The system provides a real opportunity to create parliamentary constituencies with rational and appropriate boundaries.

F2PTP-IND introduces the independent candidate into the mix. They would be a body of independently-minded people with no allegiance to political parties, yet, like most of us, with political views and personal ideological beliefs. The following shows how such a system would work in practice. Of course, the constituency boundaries would be different, but by sticking fairly closely to the constituencies we have now and combining them to create the size of constituencies the F2PTP-IND system needs, it's easier to show how things would work in practice.

I'll keep as close as I can to what we have now, just to show the mechanisms in play.

Constituency make-up

Example:

Kent.

In the current electoral system Kent has 17 Constituencies, returning 17 Members of Parliament.

Thanet North
Thanet South
Ashford
Dover
Canterbury
Folkestone and Hythe
Gillingham and Rainham
Sittingbourne and Sheppey
Faversham and Kent Mid
Rochester and Strood
Chatham and Aylesford
Maidstone and The Weald
Gravesham
Sevenoaks
Dartford
Tonbridge and Malling
Tunbridge Wells

In order to undergo the analysis of a would-be F2PTP election system for the 2015 and 2010 general elections, these constituencies were amalgamated, with one East Sussex constituency joining Tunbridge Wells. Each new constituency returned two MPs making 18 in all. Exactly the same number as before, bearing in mind that Wealden (not in Kent) returned an MP as a single constituency before.

F2PTP-IND

Kent F2PTP-IND party constituencies could look like this – 7 constituencies combined as shown:

Thanet North, Thanet South, Dover.
Ashford, Canterbury, Folkestone and Hythe.
Gillingham and Rainham, Sittingbourne and Sheppey, Faversham and Kent Mid.
Rochester and Strood, Gravesham.
Chatham and Aylesford, Maidstone and The Weald.
Sevenoaks, Dartford.
Tonbridge and Malling, Tunbridge Wells.

Each constituency would return two Party MPs making 14, plus two independent MPs. In this example the Kent County is the independent constituency. The addition of the independents would make the overall number of Kent MPs up to 16, just one less than now, but that's principally a feature of current boundaries, which would change.

Logically it could be assumed that the increased competition, two places available rather than just one, would increase voter participation. F2PTP incorporates the first and second place concepts and the Living Vote. This is where MPs vote using the number of votes they personally got in the election. F2PTP-IND is the new parliamentary structure where 512 seats are contested by parties over 256 constituencies and 128 seats are contested by independent candidates over 64 constituencies. Both sets of constituencies will elect members using the F2PTP election process. The constituencies are necessarily larger and that brings with it a new set of problems, but the voting system and its features also alleviate some problems too.

In this example we have seven party constituencies and one independent's constituency. Each voter will have two ballot papers, one for the parties and one for the independents. Voters vote exactly as they do now, by marking against the name of the person they wish to cast their vote for. One vote on the party ballot paper and one vote on the independent's ballot paper.

Voting

The votes are counted as they are now, the winner and the second placed candidates are elected in each category. In the party category the elected representatives, when voting in the House of Commons, will cast the number of votes that they received in the election. In the independent's category, each of the independents, when voting in the House of Commons, will cast the number of votes they received, divided by the number of Party constituencies that made up the independent's constituency.

Because there are two ballot papers, each voter will be casting two votes: they will be voting twice. As the ballots are together, whether sent by post or in the ballot box on the day, most people would be expected to vote on both ballot papers. This means that the total number of votes cast, normally around 32 million in a general election, will likely double to 64 million. Were the independent's real numbers of votes to be used as their House of Commons voting power then the independents as a whole would have the equivalent voting power of all the party-elected representatives, which isn't the idea. By dividing the total vote by the number of constituencies the independent's vote remains proportional to their electoral success whilst maintaining the balance that they should exercise around a quarter of the parliamentary vote.

The real voting power though will depend upon how the votes are split.

In our traditional party system and under the existing FPTP system, votes are generally cast for the Conservative Party or the Labour Party. In some constituencies where the Liberal Democrats are strong it will still be two parties contesting, the

SNP are the Liberal Democrats' main opposition in Scotland and the Conservatives in England, though one or two seats have a reasonable third place vote. We know that the lion's share of the vote will be shared between two candidates (parties) in any constituency with other candidates getting very little support and often losing deposits. (To stand for a UK parliamentary seat one must put up a £500.00 deposit which is lost if the vote share is less than 5%.)

The introduction of F2PTP will change that dynamic, as second place also becomes a win in terms of getting elected. More people are likely to support smaller parties so the voting might well be spread a little more evenly, but that tendency is also likely to be countered by more Conservative, Labour, or Liberal Democrat supporters voting, because every extra vote would count whereas extra votes under FPTP are worthless.

Interestingly, Caroline Lucas of the Green Party, a former leader, non-leader, and co-leader of the Greens, is the MP for Brighton Pavilion. In my analysis of the 2010 and 2015 general elections detailed in the F2PTP paper in the appendix and where constituencies were combined (Brighton Pavilion and Kemptown), Caroline Lucas couldn't even make second place. To confirm this anomaly, I then combined Brighton Pavilion with the other adjacent constituencies of, Hove, Arundel and South Downs, and Lewes, with the same result. Strangely, and whilst this shows minimal support for the Green Party anywhere else other than Brighton Pavilion and looks as if they would lose the only seat they have, their national options would be improved. Where Green supporters don't vote Green, they often vote Labour instead. Under the FPTP voting system the Green Party have no chance anywhere else other than Brighton Pavilion, however, under the F2PTP voting system, their votes might just yield more success when second place is in play also. Under F2PTP-IND, they may also see independent candidates standing, who might well support their ideas.

Candidates

Under our current system and broadly speaking, anyone who wishes to stand for Parliament may do so if they qualify, meaning over 18, citizenship or permanent residency and are not disqualified, i.e. police force and armed forces members, civil servants and judges, and a few other but rare disqualifications. To all intents and purposes anyone can stand. There's no limit on numbers per constituency and if you have £500.00 to lose then go for it.

We have regular frivolous candidates, a favourite being the Monster Raving Loony Party led by Howling Laud Hope, and notably in 2015 Al Murray, the comedian. Silly, yes, but exemplifying British tolerance and eccentricity and making a point. They do offer a repository for disgruntled voters and by virtue of being on the ballot paper they can indirectly send a message to the powerful.

General election ballot papers could have any number of names on them and 7 isn't unusual but rarely are there many more than that. It is delightfully self-calibrating. The nature of the FPTP voting system and the nature of the British voters means that even if there were 100 names on a ballot paper, it wouldn't affect the result at all. The pattern would remain:

- First place, lots of votes
- Second place, fewer votes but usually still lots
- Third place and below, nothing much at all

However, that wouldn't be the case for the independent vote.

It takes time for systems to bed themselves in and for people to really understand how things work. This will take several elections for people to become as familiar with F2PTP-IND as they are with FPTP. To get any change to the UK voting system a referendum would be needed with the government campaigning for the change. The precedent has already been set. These opportunities come along rarely and as I've indicated earlier, a cast iron manifesto commitment for fairer voting means absolutely nothing, so we could be in for a bit of a wait.

I'll be describing how we get from where we are now to another referendum in a later chapter, but for now, I'll consider the issues raised by an independent's ballot paper and how they can be managed.

The most obvious issue is that barring popular celebrity entrants, and the history on that isn't encouraging, voters won't know who these people are. That's not to say that people know much about their candidates now, they don't. People vote for parties, despite the self-aggrandising claims of those elected. It is likely, then, that votes would be equally split, as is wont to happen in randomised selection events, which the independent's ballot paper might well be in the early years. There are things that could be done to create some clear water between candidates, but the competition for the public's attention is severe, so I am recommending that the state provide the necessary facilities to bring the various options to the fore with a range of electoral assistance.

Currently electoral constituencies have around 70,000 voters, with the electoral lists maintained by the local authority for the parts of existing constituencies that fall within their boundaries. At the moment these areas don't always match, with constituencies spanning multiple local authorities and vice versa. These constituency numbers and areas will double under F2PTP. For the independent candidates, they will quadruple or even more as in the example above, perhaps county size.

Elections.

Typically, a general election campaign under the current system will have a national constituent and a local one. The national message is aided by TV appearances, political broadcasts and newspaper advertisements, social media and any vehicle that has a national reach. The local effort would include posters, hand-delivered leaflets, street stalls, local media, social media and canvassing. Direct phone calls can be nationally or locally done, often both. These distinct areas of expenditure are very firmly controlled, yet still abused as the Conservatives did in 2015 in the South Thanet Constituency, where they broke the law.

In 2015/16, Craig Mackinlay, the Conservative Candidate, Nathan Gray, his election agent and Marion Little who has been variously described as a party activist and party official but was in reality a Conservative Party employee since 1974, were all charged with making false declarations in connection with election expenditure for the 2015 General Election constituency of Thanet South. Both Mackinlay and Gray were acquitted whilst Little was convicted and sentenced to a 9-month suspended sentence plus a £5000.00 fine.

Election fraud and Thanet South in particular.
The above trial scratched the surface of electoral fraud. The criminal offence was knowingly making a false election expenses declaration, not the cheating itself. In order to secure a conviction, it has to be proven to the standards of the criminal law that the false declaration was made knowing it to be false. The trial was unable to prove that Mr Mackinlay and Mr Gray signed an election-expenses return without knowing what was on it. Just to reinforce this point, the Conservative Party candidate, together with his election agent (a mandatory position) submitted the defence that they weren't aware that their expenses declarations were false.

The scurrilous behaviour concerned the improper declaration of locally accrued expenses to be nationally allowed expenses because this was an election with a difference and it's worth recounting why that was, and why it is that the election law is so lax and unenforceable.

In 2015, the electoral height of UKIP, Nigel Farage was a candidate in Thanet South. The Conservative Party candidate Craig Mackinlay, ironically, a former deputy leader of UKIP from 1997 to 2000 and acting leader of UKIP in 1997, was the principal opposition. For the Conservatives this was an election they couldn't afford to lose so they spent very heavily in the constituency by bussing in activists from all over the country, boarding them in hotels in order to mount a massive campaign in this one constituency.

It is illegal to exceed the spending limits, though the charges brought weren't for overspending, they were for making a false declaration.

The expenditure connected with the bussing in of people and their accommodation expenses were clearly to the benefit of the local campaign but were declared to be national expenditure. It's not known whether the candidate or his election agent were aware of this activity.

Two important points are raised by this trial and its conclusion. The first is that cheating pays. The Conservative Party cheated outrageously, but the narrow victory of Mackinlay (2812 votes) still stood. That's like your mate stealing a car for you, being convicted but you get to keep it. Secondly, that the act of cheating itself is not prosecuted. It seems to be allowed. Prosecutions are only ever made on the technicalities such as expenses declarations which sets a very high bar indeed to prove fraud. That's one reason why there are very few convictions for this act.

Election fraud is commonly considered to be widespread but it's necessary to understand that the authorities have no interest in acknowledging that, let alone acting upon it. The pretence of election integrity must be maintained at all costs, it seems. In just the same way that the authorities failed to act in the Rotherham grooming gangs scandal, they have no wish to uncover election fraud, and when a conviction is established as in the case above, there is effectively no punishment.

In a general election, candidates also have a government funded electoral mailing, which is strictly controlled in content, size and weight. Normally, this is a single sheet, quite unimaginative and delivered by post, the printing costs are borne by the party, or candidate, but the postage is free. The party usually decide the main content and will manage the process nationally. Constituency input is limited with the constituency differences being about the candidate. When I stood in the 2017 general election for UKIP in the Rochester and Strood Constituency I used this facility in a novel way and distributed 50,000 8-page, 8000-word tabloid newspapers. I saved my deposit when all about were losing theirs, so maybe it helped. It turns out that with light paper and judicious folding and a visible imprint on the side facing upwards, a political message can be disseminated in an interesting way, with imagery and in a format that people are used to handling and reading.

Putting up posters requires hands, as does delivering leaflets, but canvassing and GOTV is by far the most labour intensive and the most effective.

Canvassing is the process whereby, in the first phase, a candidate and their team knock on doors, talk to voters, and find out who intends to vote for them. They are only interested in definite voters, not maybe, or undecided, or non-committal. The second phase is on polling day, to log everyone attending a voting booth and asking for their electoral number (not who they intend to vote for or who they have voted for). The purpose is to relay back to the party's constituency control centre, the details of who said they would vote for them and haven't yet done so. The constituency control will then phone or send a car round to the house to get out the vote (GOTV), giving lifts if necessary.

Do this well and your chances of winning are significantly increased.

For the major parties, they are helped by years of records, so they know who most of their voters are, have councillors in place who are obliged to help, so the doubling of the constituency size shouldn't make any difference as there will be twice the number of helpers.

However, for smaller parties, canvassing is virtually impossible to do properly as the resources required are substantial.

The Conservative and Labour parties are really good at this, as are the Liberal Democrats in areas where they have support. They also have more money to spend (up to the prescribed limits), so the doubling or trebling of existing constituency sizes will not make that much difference to the larger parties and it also will not make much difference to smaller parties in that they will be equally unable to compete, whatever the increased size of a constituency becomes.

The increased use of postal voting will limit the GOTV efforts, but doing that well, still pays off.

It has long been a back burner discussion as to how democracy should be financed. Currently, money talks. Large political parties are funded by donors, some small, but many large ones particularly companies. All donors expect a return. That will be either a general political direction with which they agree or more specific policies to help their businesses. It could also, of course, be just to get that knighthood or peerage.

Corrupt intent is an inherent danger of the private funding of political parties, but there has never really been any appetite for state funding from the electorate, who will have to foot the bill. It's an odd position to take when one considers the mindboggling and wasteful expenditure in the Coronavirus pandemic of 2020 and 2021.

Independents.

The independent's election though is quite a different thing.

All of the things that are done by political parties for an election cannot be done by independents. The fundamental principle of independent representation precludes private funding from any source. There's no party, no membership subscriptions, no donors, just intelligent, capable and thoughtful people to create the balance needed in our parliamentary system.

We need to address some questions:

- What is an independent candidate?
- How would the independents' electoral mechanisms help to create some clear water between people contesting a general election as independent candidates and generally unknown to the electorate?
- How many independents can stand in a constituency?

Whilst we are suggesting independent candidates that doesn't mean people with no opinions. Everyone, particularly budding parliamentarians, will be overtly political and have strong views. The independence is independence from a party machine, its selection processes and demands for loyalty, even when doing the wrong thing. So, the answers to the questions above would be:

- One who has satisfied the independence criteria
- State funded literature and media exposure in their localities
- No limit

These need a little expansion.

There is clearly a possibility for cheating, whereby people with connections to parties or close allegiances may be encouraged, or even put forward by those parties to 'pretend' independence, so there would be a declaration made by the candidate, with severe penalties for misrepresentation. I do not see this as a serious problem because the process will show any inappropriate allegiances for what they are. It could be, for example, that a prominent politician, disaffected with his party, would take this opportunity to disassociate from former party allegiance and this should not be prevented.

To discourage patronage and bribery, independent parliamentary representatives would be limited to two terms or a maximum of eight years, whichever is the greater and that maximum to only be exceeded to see the end of the current parliamentary session. They would not be eligible for ministerial office, nor would they be entitled to honours dispensed by patronage, but instead would be a part of a people's list for recognition when their term had ended. This is not a position for a career-minded or hugely ambitious person; it is for people who want to contribute. On the plus side they will be paid very well and receive a substantial pension on leaving office. This shouldn't be a position for the already rich, but they shouldn't be excluded either. Independents would be required on parliamentary committees in any position, and they could act as speaker if parliament so wished.

To explain the terms of service:

- Two five-year parliaments, equals ten years, fine.
- One three-year parliament and one five-year parliament, equals eight years and also fine.
- One three-year parliament followed by a four-year parliament followed by a five-year parliament, equals twelve years, also fine.

As long as the third (or fourth, or fifth etc.) parliament begins before the eight-year limit is reached then the independent will continue to serve until that parliament ends.

Independent candidates would cover large geographical areas, so they will not be able to deliver to each house, nor will they be able to canvass or get out the vote, nor will they have a manifesto for government or any national exposure. The following aid should be provided.

- A postal message of introduction at the beginning of the campaign. A statement of personal beliefs one week later, and a reminder to vote, to postal voters, the same day that the ballot papers are posted and the day before polling day to non-postal voters. All of these documents to be prepared and submitted with the candidacy nominations.
- A website for each constituency where each candidate can present both video and written submissions and where their interviews and debates would be available.
- A candidate office staffed by local authority staff to receive and pass on messages and respond. Also, to maintain the independent's constituency website. The administrative office would remain in place for the elected independent representatives.
- Two televised debates (local TV) between constituency independent candidates and one forensic interview for each candidate, all of which will be available on the website.

By these means every voter will have the opportunity to assess each person in a process that would be substantially more informative than any election material you have ever been bombarded with. In UK elections, nobody votes for a person, they vote for a party, despite what the politicians like to pretend. In this election people will be voting for a person.

By these means we will establish a parliament with the largest party forming the government and able to pursue its agenda. To pass legislation, the government would need to persuade a proportion of the independent vote to back them. They will not be able to coerce or bribe independent votes with promises of ministerial jobs or future honours; persuasion will have to be by debate. They will not have an overall majority, cannot act in a dictatorial manner, and will not be subject to automatic opposition or political games as would befall a minority government under the present system.

In the unlikely event of the two main parties achieving the same voting power (remembering that it is no longer about seats, but votes received), then the choice of government would be put to the House. In the even more unlikely scenario that the House vote is also tied, then there would be another election.

True democracy must also include limits on the use of power. The independents might well be the most important body in a revised and much more representative parliament.

Chapter Summary.

F2PTP-IND is a hybrid voting system, simple in operation, which uses the F2PTP method of first and second place winners as well as a prescribed number of independent and regionally based MPs. The idea is to create an elected body of MPs in Parliament who are not beholden to any vested interests. Not parties, not donors, not corruptible. They would be the guardians of our democracy.

The next chapter:

Describes how such reform could be achieved. It is probably the most important chapter.

All the worth of an idea falls to nought if not enacted.

Chapter 7

The Way Forward?

The Brexit strategy was as follows.

Take a popular item, campaign repeatedly and recruit members and supporters, contest elections and after many years build significant support. It's unlikely that there will be enough support nationwide to win a seat, because for a national issue, support is likely to be evenly spread throughout the country, whereas to win seats one needs it condensed into small areas. Except, that is, for the Conservative and Labour parties who have enough votes to win in most constituencies.

It's important to recognise the durability of brand. Most people do not vote for the individual named on the ballot paper, but for the party they represent. They also do not vote for the contents of manifestos, because few ever bother to read them, so the driving force is a combination of brand, general allegiance based on which camp one feels more comfortable being in and the personality of the respective leaders. I'm not suggesting that there aren't other factors as well, but the vote in UK general elections is predominantly shared between the Conservative and Labour parties, regardless of manifestos, competence, corruption, and even criminality. It is pretty well set in stone. No existing party can break this mould, even those like the Liberal Democrats, or the Greens who have existed for a long time but still have minuscule national support. They are too well known, their place in national politics is set, and all they can expect are small fluctuations in their vote, but never enough to make a difference.

As time goes on, the stereotypes of the parties harden, entirely due to the electoral system and the duality it maintains. The Conservatives are cast as financially competent, tax reducing,

The Living Vote

corrupt and uncaring and only in it for themselves. The Labour Party is cast as financially incompetent, borrowing too much, wanting the state to run your entire life, putting up taxes and gesture politics. In a nutshell, the nasty party versus the incompetent party. In moments of rationality many see through this with the disappointing reality that there's nothing much between them in terms of ideology or competence or anything else.

Their overriding objective is simply to win power.

The evidence we have clearly shows that new parties are doomed to failure despite having comprehensive manifestos, often quite good ones with which many would agree, but not vote for. Contesting elections, against two parties with an established vote, on the same political ground and competing under rules they set and control, is never going to work. It's worth looking at some serious attempts to do this.

The Gang of Four in 1981, consisting of David Owen (Foreign Secretary), Roy Jenkins (Deputy Leader of the Labour Party), Bill Rodgers (Transport Secretary) and Shirley Williams (Education Secretary and Paymaster General), left the Labour Party and started a new party called The Social Democrats. By any description, these were political big hitters, highly educated, thoughtful, and brilliant politicians with a huge national profile and with a background of the Labour Party which had significant support and political power.

However, in the 1983 and 1987 general elections they stood as the Liberal/SDP Alliance with terrible results and after the 1987 election merged fully with the Liberal party to form the Liberal Democrats which remains today, but even smaller, in the sense of a parliamentary presence, than they were in 1987.

The second significant and much more successful political emergence was UKIP, which began life as the Anti-Federalist League under Alan Sked, in 1991. It was renamed UKIP in 1993. In 1997 Nigel Farage took over as leader and progressively

84

improved the party's electoral standing. Substantial inroads to electoral success were achieved in the 2013 local elections.

Nigel Farage is a larger-than-life character and although he broadened the argument to challenge uncontrolled immigration and incorporated a full policy range for government, a parliamentary presence eluded the party, until much later when two Conservative MPs, Douglas Carswell and Mark Reckless, swapped allegiances, resigned their seats and won them back as UKIP MPs in 2014.

In 2015, UKIP, whilst having massive success in the EU elections, which was to continue, also had their best-ever general election success, yet still only retained the Clacton constituency with Douglas Carswell, their only remaining MP.

These two examples represent the best successes of new political parties. The SDP on the one hand, with a huge profile and political big hitters, failed abysmally, and UKIP, with over 20 years of building behind it and huge national support as was consistently demonstrated in repeated EU elections, local elections and the 2016 referendum, still couldn't break the mould.

The message, or perhaps the reality is clear. In the UK, change brought about by a new political force with intention of winning parliamentary power is not going to happen all the while we have the FPTP voting system, but that's where we are.

Whilst UKIP could not set the agenda with parliamentary presence, the party did drive the biggest constitutional change since 1973, when the UK said yes to a trading arrangement then called the Common Market. That became the European Union and UKIP's years of opposition to this federalist organisation culminated in the 2016 EU referendum when the UK decided to leave.

UKIP was a single-issue party. Subordinate concerns such as immigration required that the primary concern be enacted, to leave the EU. Policies on the economy, security, defence, education were seen as being controlled by the creep of EU law. Everything depended on the one principal act, that of leaving the EU.

We now have a similar fundamental single issue. Nothing can change in our political system or the effectiveness of government until the people are better represented, and governance has a much broader support than is possible with our current system.

Change this, change everything.

Significant national support for a party doesn't win seats in Parliament, and therefore change cannot be brought about that way though support is still hugely influential, and that support is often expressed in votes. Votes that would have otherwise been cast for another party, and this is where the power can be indirectly applied.

The UKIP result of 2010 was an indicator of the potential threat when they got just under a million votes. The then Prime Minister, David Cameron, having failed to gain an overall majority, clearly saw the potential for this threat to grow, but also to enhance his party's electoral position. On 23rd January 2013 he announced that there would be an in/out referendum on Britain's continued membership of the European Union, no later than the end of 2017.

From David Cameron's perspective this was a rational decision. He was aware that many Labour supporters were also supporters of the leave EU cause, whereas the Labour Party was rabidly Europhile in nature. He would, in one fell swoop, shoot UKIP's fox, and he knew that governments always win referendums. The perfect solution.

As it happened the 2015 general election result made this referendum an absolute certainty. It is not beyond the realms of possibility that, had UKIP's support fallen dramatically, David Cameron would have found a way to avoid holding it. Then again, governments always win referendums, so he really didn't see any risk.

However, the die was cast when UKIP polled 3.8 million votes in the 2015 general election. There was no way the Prime Minister could wiggle out of it as the UKIP campaign reminded people that it's not yet done and that a big vote for UKIP would ensure that the referendum would take place.

The EU referendum, then, was forced onto the government by the weight of support for a single issue. UKIP had no chance of being the government, or of even winning Parliamentary seats in any number, yet this long-term organisation with constituency associations around the country and a powerful single issue won the biggest constitutional change in 50 years. It was a monumental success for UKIP and Nigel Farage in particular.

Getting it done, however, would take another four years, and the issue dominated the 2017 general election, along with the 'not Corbyn at any cost' campaign messaging. Brexit also dominated the 2019 general election when Boris Johnson won a substantial majority with the Brexit issue still prominent.

To achieve this, it took UKIP 25 years to build the necessary structure and with a clear and unambiguous message. UKIP campaigned relentlessly, contested all elections, and repeatedly expressed the concerns of ordinary working people with the restrictions and rules imposed by our expensive membership of this European Union. It took a while, so there is no reason to imagine that voting reform will be any easier or any quicker, particularly if those that support this massive constitutional change continue to focus their attention on activity that demonstrably cannot make any progress. As mentioned before, as far as this issue is concerned, we haven't moved forward at all.

So, why then, when there are clear examples of what doesn't work and what does work, do supporters of voting reform not do what works?

So how do we do this?

The first option I'll discuss and the one preferred by the reform supporting organisations, as far as I can gather, is to convince the government that voting reform is needed and get them either to legislate directly to introduce it or to hold a referendum on it.

This approach has some quite obvious problems and some not so obvious ones.

- When I say government, I mean a Labour government because the Conservatives will never change their own winning formula. The first problem therefore is, we don't have a Labour government.
- Even when the next Labour government is elected, they will have won under the existing system, so why would they want to change it? This is exactly what happened in 1997. If they lose another couple of elections, the probability of electoral reform will again become a commitment, so ironically our best chance of getting these changes via this method depends upon the Conservatives winning, at least, the next election.
- When a Labour government is next elected, and it will happen, and if they do decide on electoral reform, it will likely be via a referendum, which they may support or oppose. A commitment for a referendum is a perfect way out of the conundrum of being forced to address the issue, but not really wanting any change. They may well do a Cameron and oppose it. If the government opposes it, they will specifically choose a system that will be defeated. Remember 2011.
- If they put any of the existing and/or preferred election systems to a referendum, they will certainly be defeated if the government campaigns against. If they campaign for, then it might succeed, but it will not resolve the

fundamental problems of all powerful governments.

- If they simply decide to introduce a more proportional voting system it won't be F2PTP-IND, therefore it won't solve the principal problems of coalition governments.
- Parliamentarians will never support the F2PTP-IND system because it puts half of them out of a job.

The second option is best, but even longer term.

This option doesn't require the agreement of the very parties we want to kick out of absolute power, which is a real advantage, because whatever they might say neither the Labour Party, nor the Conservative Party wants such a change. It will, however, take time.

The campaign could use one of the existing parties, like UKIP for example, or perhaps Reform UK, which has a real benefit in having Nigel Farage involved. However, their electoral attempts so far have been disastrous, and they seem more interested in short-term issues that, whilst on the public's mind today, will be gone tomorrow. It's possible the government will shoot their fox before they have time to feed it up!

It cannot be said often or loud enough that voting reform is the biggest issue of our time. Change that, change everything.

This is the way to do it.

Set up a political party with one overriding purpose; for UKIP it was Brexit, for this new party it must be voting reform. Voting reform is a part of overall electoral reform, but the concepts of voting reform are much easier to sell and explain. The rebirth of The Brexit Party is Reform UK, and they support electoral reform, but aren't taking advantage of the purpose of a single-issue political idea.

For the sake of a name, let's call this political party the Fairer Voting Party. Reform UK have made a terrible mistake. They are pretending to be a political party with a chance of government, whereas in elections they lose deposits. The Fairer Voting Party isn't principally interested in being in government, or even winning seats; it will have two clear objectives.

- To educate the public on the effect of the F2PTP-IND voting system and House of Commons structure. People do understand what's wrong, they endure the effects of inflation, rising prices, involvement in wars, and they know the politicians are responsible, but few understand how the structure of our electoral system underpins the defective governments we get, and how much of an improvement such a system will bring. There needs to be years of debate and a constant repetition of real benefits, such as the Living Vote. We need to connect the failures of our electoral system to the abuses it allows and the political and social problems it brings. Fixing this is a priority, but it will take time.
- To gain mass support for fairer voting the party will need to establish constituency associations nationwide. To register real support through votes, a party has to have candidates in each constituency. This also will take time.

This single issue does have a major advantage in that it isn't controversial. Most people would support fairer voting with only politicians and their parties opposed. F2PTP-IND removes the untrammelled power they can wield, limits the patronage they can bestow and holds them in check. That's exactly what the people want and exactly what our political elite do not. Brexit was divisive, fairer voting isn't. It's effectively the people versus the politicians, and the people have to win.

The first step in this process then is to fully explain what is wrong and describe in detail how to fix it, which is what this book is all about. The new political party will be for others to pursue, with success probably 20 years away, and it is quite likely that I'll not be here to see it.

Support is the critical ingredient, followed up by real votes. It isn't just about taking votes away from the two parties who are vying for power. It's actually easier than that, because to send a message, they only need people to have an intention to vote for them. The polls will do the rest. In the UK, change only happens through voting, not protests, so voting and the intention to vote are key.

Such a party would benefit from a well-known and influential figurehead, but principally it must focus on the voting reform arguments so that when the referendum is conceded, it will be won. That cannot be done from the basis of existing political parties as they already have political history and are usually factored into any electoral calculations. For example, the Liberal Democrats will win some seats, sometimes more sometimes less, but either way it's irrelevant. Their last high point was in 2010, but still we had a majority Conservative government.

At the time of writing, and by way of example, Nigel Farage, the president of Reform UK, is starting a campaign for a net zero referendum. I know that by the time you read this it will be ancient history, and that's the point. It's a current political topic, which will wane, giving no time to educate people in a way that will elicit their long-term support. It can also be torpedoed instantly, by the government watering the Net Zero targets down a bit, or conceding a referendum, but unlike Brexit which took many years to get the kind of support that would make a difference, Net Zero is just today's topic and can be gone in an instant. Being successful in either getting the government to change its position or grant a referendum ends the campaign.

Voting reform is by far the biggest issue of our time. Get that and everything changes.

Earlier, I alluded to the lack of progress from all the organisations promoting voting reform and the difficulty in getting anything substantial from years of campaigning, because there is no mechanism to coalesce support in a meaningful way.

In real terms and after years of what has to be described as pointless activity, nothing has changed, and nothing looks even remotely like changing.

Our theoretical single-issue party needs a single-issue which is long term, and which fundamentally changes the political landscape when achieved. The Fairer Voting Party needs time to present and explain the benefits of the proposals, just as people needed constant reminders of how bad, expensive, controlling and unreasonable the EU is, to cement that support so that it shows up in opinion polls and votes.

In order to educate, to sell and to explain a new voting system, and to get people to vote for it, it has to exist. It has to be a system, fully explainable, debatable, significant parts of it need to be easily and readily expressed, memorable, and repeatable with pertinent slogans. Whilst this all sounds necessary, there is a body of opinion that just wants agreement to PR in principle, no detail, just leave that to the government and they'll decide. How do you sell that in a referendum?

There is a great freedom in creating and expressing ideas. There isn't enough of that in our society today and people have lost the ability to evaluate and consider new ideas, particularly if they don't come from within their own pre-approved circle. However, none of it matters because in time more people will see that our political class are only interested in wielding and increasing their power over and at the expense of the people. When enough people see this, we will reset our democracy to work for us.

Thank you for reading. I hope it has been interesting and stimulated your thoughts.

Chapter Summary.

There are only two ways of getting a change to our voting system. Get the Labour Party to commit to it and hope they follow through or attract electoral support through the only mechanism that can do this, a political party.

Appendix 1

F2PTP
First Two Past the Post

A VOTING SYSTEM FOR EQUALITY OF REPRESENTATION
IN A MULTIPARTY STATE

Time for Change.

In 2010, 29,687,604 people voted. The Conservatives received 10,703,654, the Labour Party 8,606,517 and the Liberal Democrats 6,836,248 with the remaining 3,541,185 shared amongst the other parties. That translated to a voting power in the legislature of 306, 258, 57, and 29 seats respectively.

The Liberal Democrats required four times the support of Labour per parliamentary vote.

In 2015 the situation became even less representative:

- SNP   < 1.5 million votes = 56 seats
- UKIP   > 3.8 million votes = 1 seat

This distortion of representation cannot be allowed to continue.

A fair yet pragmatic voting system needs to adhere to some fundamental principles.

- It must be simple to understand for the electorate and transparent in operation. All current PR systems fail to meet such criteria.
- An elected representative must retain a direct connection with the constituents that elected them. This underpins the authority of a representative and allows for recall (sacking) by the very constituents that gave that authority to begin with. All current PR systems fail on this point, at least in part.
- Parliamentary power should accurately reflect the wishes of all the people and not just a fortunately placed minority. FPTP fails spectacularly in this respect.
- Very small parties or geographically limited parties should be excluded from representation. FPTP achieves this to the point of excluding major parties, but most PR systems depend upon some arbitrary pre-definition of success to

do this. F2PTP incorporates this aspect automatically. Second place works, third place doesn't.

- Constituency boundaries and size of electorate should not be overly significant. Whilst it makes sense to retain some uniformity it makes even more sense to align constituencies with existing governmental structures such as counties or regions. FPTP requires some strange boundary configurations to attempt equality of electorate size which would cease to be an issue.

Any system that can meet all the above criteria must be worth a look.

The Fundamental Flaws of FPTP.

FPTP has been the voting system used in the UK for many years and has some benefit where only two main parties contest an election. When in a multiparty state the system breaks down and disenfranchises the majority of voters who see no possibility of achieving representation. The overall effect of this is to contribute to the alienation of people and discourage involvement.

FPTP encourages the marginalisation of many parts of the country. Ironically, the vast majority of electoral local effort goes to 'marginal seats' thereby ignoring those seats where the majority is seen to be unshakable. Not only do 'safe' seats lose out from party and government attention democracy itself is the loser when the marginal constituencies always decide the outcome.

An aspect of FPTP, because of its propensity to overly advantage geographical enclaves, is the encouragement and real increase in sectarian movements as seen with the SNP. Despite the appearance of overwhelming support, the reality is very different. Only 1,454,436 people in Scotland voted for the

SNP out of a population of 5.3 million and an electorate of 4.2 million.

Only the distortion provided by the FPTP system could display this result as an overwhelming statement of support. Most Scots voted against the SNP, but their views were nullified by a system that artificially created a disproportionate outcome.

Sectarianism and division always lead to extreme behaviour once a certain tipping point has been reached. One might think that it would be in the best interests of a country to avoid creating such situations yet the self-serving nature of the two main parties are content to allow such disparity to grow because they believe that the distortion apparent in this election benefits them enormously and the nature of party politics in the 21st century seems to value the maintenance of political power above all other considerations. It is surprising then that in the 2015 election Labour would have done better under the F2PTP system than FPTP.

The F2PTP system, described below, resolves all of these aspects. Perhaps it's worth some consideration?

A Summary.

- F2PTP is a voting system that selects both the winner and the second placed candidates in a constituency parliamentary election.
- The MPs selected by this method vote in parliament with the actual numbers of votes cast for them directly in the said election.

As it happens the inclusion of second place automatically creates a degree of proportionality whilst still requiring a bar to be overcome (see the votes per seat calculations below).

There are 650 members of Parliament, 533 in England, 59 in Scotland, 40 in Wales and 18 in Northern Ireland. By merging every two adjacent constituencies into one new F2PTP constituency the number of MPs remains almost the same. The actual number will be 648 because of the odd numbers of constituencies in England and Scotland requiring two new F2PTP constituencies to be made up of six former ones. Each MP will retain equality of representation, status and opportunity so as far as the constituency elector is concerned, they remain equal in their representational roles. The F2PTP system is not affected by any subsequent re-definition of boundaries for any reason and still works well.

Voting in Parliament, however, will change. The outdated and quaint system of passing through to a lobby has massive disadvantages and is no longer suited to the modern world. In voting matters the representative will lose the existing and artificial equality within the legislature, which is part of the current system, and change to a proportional one. If MP1 was elected with 10,000 votes and MP2 with 20,000 they will remain the numbers of votes they individually cast in parliament every time a vote is taken. This way your vote counts for the duration of the parliament.

By these means representatives retain a constituency association and equality of direct representation yet exercise their proportional support within the legislative process. An individual vote of a successful first or second placed candidate would no longer be discarded immediately after the election result, but be cast again and again in every parliamentary vote.

This simple, feasible and practical system is relatively easy to implement and provides some remarkable and not immediately apparent progress in widening representation and making the political process more relevant to the people.

If more people get what they vote for more may well engage with the process.

The Effect – 2015 FPTP.

The 2015 effect on principle electoral measurements is as follows.

FPTP the current system.

30,674,959	Votes cast.
15,339,995	Voters got the representative they voted for.
7,461,407	Votes were wasted by being in excess of the required number to secure first place.
15,335,614	Votes were wasted or ineffective by being cast for unsuccessful candidates.

Party	SumOfVote	Seats	Votes Per Seat	% Total Vote
Conservative	11,325,531	331	34216	36.9211%
Labour	9,347,304	232	40290	30.4721%
UKIP	3,876,674	1	3876674	12.6379%
Liberal Democrat	2,415,862	8	301983	7.8757%
SNP	1,454,436	56	25972	4.7414%
Green	1,155,375	1	1155375	3.7665%
DUP	184,260	8	23033	0.6007%
Alliance	61,556	0		0.2007%
Sinn Fein	176,232	4	44058	0.5745%
UUP	114,935	2	57468	0.3747%
SDLP	99,809	3	33270	0.3254%
Plaid Cymru	181,704	3	60568	0.5924%
Others	281,281	1	281281	0.9170%
Total	30,674,959	650		

Overall majority required 326 seats, achieved.

If the F2PTP system were to be introduced for the 2020 general election 325 MPs would be guaranteed to lose their seats. Whilst this is not likely to find support with the group whose self-interest may be a significant factor, it may well be just what the public would like to see. It is less likely to provide a government with an overall majority.

F2PTP the proposed system.

30,674,959	Votes cast.
22,778,475	Voters would have got the representative they voted for.
0	Votes would have been wasted by being in excess of what was required.
7,896,484	Votes would have been wasted or ineffective by being cast for unsuccessful candidates.

Party	SumOfVote	Seats	Votes Per Seat	% Total Vote
Conservative	11,325,531	265	42738	36.9211%
Labour	9,347,304	253	36946	30.4721%
UKIP	3,876,674	45	86148	12.6379%
Liberal Democrat	2,415,862	33	73208	7.8757%
SNP	1,454,436	29	50153	4.7414%
Green	1,155,375	0		3.7665%
DUP	184,260	7	26323	0.6007%
Alliance	61,556	2	30778	0.2007%
Sinn Fein	176,232	4	44058	0.5745%
UUP	114,935	3	38312	0.3747%
SDLP	99,809	2	49905	0.3254%
Plaid Cymru	181,704	4	45426	0.5924%
Others	281,281	1	281281	0.9170%
Total	30,674,959	648		

Overall majority required 15,337,480 votes; not achieved.
Conservative, UKIP, DUP = 15,386,465 = Majority.

The Main Factors 2015 F2PTP.

- Constituency MPs remain accountable to their constituents.
- A third more voters get the representative they voted for.
- There are less than a third of the wasted votes under FPTP.
- The votes per MP/Seat are much more even.
- Voting power in the commons is directly proportional to votes cast.
- When a vote is cast it remains active throughout the parliament.
- It would have benefitted the Labour Party as well as Liberal Democrats and UKIP.

The Effect 2010.

The 2010 effect on principle electoral measurements is as follows.

FPTP the current system.

14,002,295   Voters got the representative they voted for.

5,438,510   Votes were wasted by being in excess of the required number to secure first place.

15,684,659   Votes were wasted or ineffective by being cast for unsuccessful candidates.

Party	SumOfVote	Seats	Votes Per Seat	% Total Vote
Conservative	10,703,654	306	34979	36.0543%
Labour	8,606,517	258	33359	28.9903%
Liberal Democrat	6,836,248	57	119934	23.0273%
Others	3,541,185	29	122110	11.9282%

Overall majority required 326 seats, not achieved.

F2PTP the proposed system.

20,727,717   Voters would have got the representative they voted for.

0   Votes would have been wasted by being in excess of what was required.

8,959,239   Votes would have been wasted or ineffective by being cast for unsuccessful candidates.

Party	SumOfVote	Seats	Votes Per Seat	% Total Vote
Conservative	10,703,654	248	43160	36.0543%
Labour	8,606,517	213	40406	28.9903%
Liberal Democrat	6,836,248	149	45881	23.0273%
Others	3,541,185	38	93189	11.9282%

Overall majority required 14,843,803 votes, not achieved.

The Overall Effect of F2PTP.

- One and a half times as many voters would get the representative they voted for.
- A third less wasted votes.
- Every successful vote would count throughout the parliament again and again.
- Votes per seat are virtually equalised for the main parties.
- No longer could there be overwhelming sectarian enclaves based on geographical or nationalistic factors.
- Tactical voting becomes irrelevant.
- A majority government is still perfectly possible but would have greater moral legitimacy.
- Were a coalition to be required its make-up would likely be more evident before voting began.
- Constituency boundaries become irrelevant in terms of size of electorate thereby easier to match them to naturally occurring or existing governmental boundaries.
- The concept of 'marginal seats' becomes much more difficult to rationalise. In the F2PTP scenario most seats could be described as 'marginal'.
- Success attracts! Better quality officials, members and candidates are attracted to causes that are more likely to be successful.

Because of the inclusion of second placed candidates, parties that have a spread of support nationally will generally do better than localised or nationalistic parties. It also has the effect of spreading the colours. No longer will the south be only blue but blue, purple, red and yellow. This applies almost everywhere even Scotland where current levels of SNP support are unusually high.

Quite unexpectedly the parties who would benefit from this system, were it to have been in place for the 2015 election, would include Labour. Clearly it provides better representation for Liberal Democrats and UKIP as expected but not for the Greens showing that their success in Brighton Pavilion is highly localised and doesn't extend to even neighbouring constituencies.

As well as the numerical improvements one has to consider that the extension of representation as delivered by the F2PTP system may well encourage future participation in the electoral process by simply giving a voice to those permanently disenfranchised by the current system.

Today, 'why bother to vote' is an arguable concept, after all most votes will be unsuccessful and discarded. This most simple and transparent of systems changes almost all of that.

A significant factor would be a change in voting habit. Whereas people may well have regarded a vote for a smaller party such as the Liberal Democrats, or currently UKIP, they may well revise their views to reflect the reality that, as second places count, a protest vote may no longer be just a protest.

This is likely to sharpen the minds of smaller parties and encourage them to become more professional and electable rather than adopt a negative and undefined position simply to attract the disaffected. This would be a good thing. A campaign content of 'vote for us because you don't like them' loses traction and becomes vote for us because of what we stand for and what we would want to achieve.

With any change there are unforeseen effects, but because this comparison has been applied over two elections with similar outcomes there should not be too many surprises.

We must be aware though, that voting behaviour will most probably change with a more egalitarian system like F2PTP but perhaps that can only be a good thing.

Importantly the system avoids the obvious accusation that it is only being promoted because it benefits X, Y, or Z. Sometimes one has to do the right thing because it is the right thing to do and not be driven by self-interest. All PR systems would have the effect of benefitting the smaller parties, far greater than the F2PTP system described here. Opposition underpinned by such argument would, therefore, be much less effective.

By-elections.

Every electoral system has to have a mechanism to replace representatives mid-term. One benefit of the current FPTP system is that this process is simple, there is a by-election. It is simply a case of one out and one in. Proportional systems like STV and Party List systems, and F2PTP can't do that because the other MP/s is/are still in place, so some other mechanism needs to be put in place to replace MPs who do not see out their term.

For F2PTP-IND and the party elections the party will simply replace the MP who has left with a nominee. In cases of MPs wishing to cross the floor, they would be required to stand down from their seat and wait until the next election to stand again. For the independents there will be an election under FPTP rules as only one candidate will be replaced. Other proportional systems have a plethora of mechanisms to deal with MPs who fail to see out their elected term for the party they originally stood for.

About the Author

Like most people, my life was pretty ordinary, being concerned principally with my family and my work, and apart from an interest in news, and being a regular voter, I didn't pay too much attention to active politics. After all, that was stuff other people did.

Around 2011, I began to show a little more interest. I had, at that time, retired almost completely. I had completed my book *The Sophisticated Alcoholic*, a very different way of dealing with alcohol dependency issues, citing the reasons for such behaviour, and providing options for permanent change. I had previously written a chapter in the Newton Institute book *Memories of the Afterlife*, which has since sold over a million copies, so had pretty well achieved what I wanted in my role as a therapist and regression hypnotherapist so together with my personal issues, it was time to retire fully, and politics just seemed to be there waiting.

What drove me was incredulity about government incompetence. The lying, misrepresentation, ill thought-out policies, and the general tardiness of our political class left me dumbfounded. My thinking then, as it is now, is that I can do better, so I began to play a more active part in the political scene. Having been disenchanted with the conceptually laudable, but practically dysfunctional European Union, I joined UKIP and began to help where I could. Personal issues still prevailed. A principal reason for retiring from work was to care for my wife, who had been diagnosed with breast cancer at the end of 2008 and was weakening. My political activities were limited because of my home role, but I did what I could, in designing leaflets and going to the odd meeting.

UKIP were going through a very successful stage, largely because of the Brexit flagship policy, and in 2016, when my wife passed and after the funeral, I became involved in the referendum campaign by way of distraction and keeping busy. After June 6th, I spent some time out of the country for space and reflection as my life had changed immeasurably. To help with the referendum campaign I wrote an 8-page tabloid newspaper which extolled the benefits of Brexit in a way that leaflets just cannot do. We had 60,000 copies printed and had them delivered through Kent, Surrey and Sussex. From comments made by those to whom we spoke after the newspapers had been delivered, they had been received very well.

At the end of 2016 I stood in a borough council by-election, which I lost, county council elections the following May, which I lost and a parliamentary election that year which, yes you guessed it. At least I saved my deposit which was a rarity in 2017. Later in 2017, I stood for the leadership of UKIP and campaigned throughout the country. Partway through I decided to step down, after all I wanted a voice, I couldn't win, but I backed the person who did win, Henry Bolton. I was appointed as spokesperson for electoral reform and joined the UKIP cabinet, albeit briefly.

The current electoral system is grossly unfair, and I've been on the receiving end of it as has UKIP and other smaller parties on many occasions. The boat, had there been one after the 2015 general election, seemed to have been missed. In that election UKIP gained 3,881,099 votes and one seat. The SNP got 1,454,435 votes and 56 seats. The Liberal Democrats got 2,415,916 votes and 8 seats whilst the Greens got 1,157,630 votes and 1 seat. The unfairness, not to parties or to party leaders, but to voters was palpable. However, such things are short-lived in the minds of the electorate.

I had been working for a while on a revised voting system that didn't have the considerable drawbacks of conventional 'PR' systems, which were typically ultra-complicated, loved by geeks, reassigned votes and gerrymandered a result that is claimed to be 'proportional', as far as that is a desirable characteristic. It was a laborious task to put the 2010 and 2015 results through the system to produce an alternative set of would-have-been results. I challenged people on many forums to break the system, to tell me what was wrong, but to my surprise, even those who professed to support fairer voting were only interested in advancing their own pet preference. New ideas weren't received well, which is not unusual, but on the upside, nobody could fault the F2PTP system.

Later in 2017, as I have already indicated, in what was an optimistic move at best, I contested the UKIP leadership election when Paul Nuttall had stood down after UKIP's poor general election result. Mad because UKIP demanded a £5000.00 deposit, plus an additional £1000.00 for an entry in the national magazine, all of which came from savings. However, I wanted a voice, I wanted to raise the profile of electoral reform, I wanted to put forward UKIP policies, which were good, in a voter acceptable manner, and travelled the country until mid-August, when I had a conversation.

A late entrant into this leadership election was Henry Bolton. I had met him once before when he was standing for the PCC elections in Kent and was aware of his background. To be blunt, the field for the leadership election in 2017 was weak, and it seemed that it might go to the person with the highest profile. However, Henry's background and general demeanour made him a strong candidate.

As I said, I entered this contest to have a voice, which I did. It transpired that I may be able to extend that voice, were Henry to win, which I thought he would, so I called him, and we discussed the campaign, ideas and political positioning and we found ourselves in general agreement. I offered to step down and support him which must have helped because it made the news and was reported as a boost to Henry's campaign. For me, I wanted to pursue and develop a policy for UKIP on electoral reform to which he agreed were he to win. After his victory, as the UKIP spokesperson for electoral reform and UKIP cabinet member and for a few months before the castle tumbled, I had drafted, together with a group of volunteers, a comprehensive electoral policy in manifesto shape. Whilst it was completed it never saw approval as the regime had changed again and such a role wasn't seen as necessary. The focus of UKIP had veered sharply toward an anti-Islam party and electoral suicide.

I've written many articles on electoral reform since and I am still sure that it can be implemented in such a way as to maintain those aspects that are so critical to voter acceptance.

It's taken 5 years for the final piece of the jigsaw to fall into place and maybe that time was needed, but the wait has been worthwhile in my view. However, you'll be the judge of that.

The concepts are too long for an article, too complex for a podcast, so I decided to write this book. It is my gift to the political arena, and I hope it opens a path towards a better electoral infrastructure, a better parliament and better legislation.

O-BOOKS

SPIRITUALITY

O is a symbol of the world, of oneness and unity; this eye represents knowledge and insight. We publish titles on general spirituality and living a spiritual life. We aim to inform and help you on your own journey in this life.
If you have enjoyed this book, why not tell other readers by posting a review on your preferred book site?

Recent bestsellers from O-Books are:

Heart of Tantric Sex
Diana Richardson
Revealing Eastern secrets of deep love and intimacy to Western couples.
Paperback: 978-1-90381-637-0 ebook: 978-1-84694-637-0

Crystal Prescriptions
The A-Z guide to over 1,200 symptoms and their healing crystals
Judy Hall
The first in the popular series of eight books, this handy little guide is packed as tight as a pill-bottle with crystal remedies for ailments.
Paperback: 978-1-90504-740-6 ebook: 978-1-84694-629-5

Take Me To Truth
Undoing the Ego
Nouk Sanchez, Tomas Vieira
The best-selling step-by-step book on shedding the Ego, using the teachings of *A Course In Miracles*.
Paperback: 978-1-84694-050-7 ebook: 978-1-84694-654-7

The 7 Myths about Love...Actually!
The Journey from your HEAD to the HEART of your SOUL
Mike George
Smashes all the myths about LOVE.
Paperback: 978-1-84694-288-4 ebook: 978-1-84694-682-0

The Holy Spirit's Interpretation of the New Testament
A Course in Understanding and Acceptance
Regina Dawn Akers
Following on from the strength of *A Course In Miracles*, NTI teaches us how to experience the love and oneness of God.
Paperback: 978-1-84694-085-9 ebook: 978-1-78099-083-5

The Message of A Course In Miracles
A translation of the Text in plain language
Elizabeth A. Cronkhite
A translation of *A Course In Miracles* into plain, everyday language for anyone seeking inner peace. The companion volume, *Practicing A Course In Miracles*, offers practical lessons and mentoring.
Paperback: 978-1-84694-319-5 ebook: 978-1-84694-642-4

Your Simple Path
Find Happiness in every step
Ian Tucker
A guide to helping us reconnect with what is really important in our lives.
Paperback: 978-1-78279-349-6 ebook: 978-1-78279-348-9

365 Days of Wisdom
Daily Messages To Inspire You Through The Year
Dadi Janki
Daily messages which cool the mind, warm the heart and guide you along your journey.
Paperback: 978-1-84694-863-3 ebook: 978-1-84694-864-0

Body of Wisdom
Women's Spiritual Power and How it Serves
Hilary Hart
Bringing together the dreams and experiences of women across the world with today's most visionary spiritual teachers.
Paperback: 978-1-78099-696-7 ebook: 978-1-78099-695-0

Dying to Be Free
From Enforced Secrecy to Near Death to True Transformation
Hannah Robinson
After an unexpected accident and near-death experience, Hannah Robinson found herself radically transforming her life, while a remarkable new insight altered her relationship with her father, a practising Catholic priest.
Paperback: 978-1-78535-254-6 ebook: 978-1-78535-255-3

The Ecology of the Soul
A Manual of Peace, Power and Personal Growth for Real People
in the Real World
Aidan Walker
Balance your own inner Ecology of the Soul to regain your
natural state of peace, power and wellbeing.
Paperback: 978-1-78279-850-7 ebook: 978-1-78279-849-1

Not I, Not other than I
The Life and Teachings of Russel Williams
Steve Taylor, Russel Williams
The miraculous life and inspiring teachings of one of the World's
greatest living Sages.
Paperback: 978-1-78279-729-6 ebook: 978-1-78279-728-9

On the Other Side of Love
A woman's unconventional journey towards wisdom
Muriel Maufroy
When life has lost all meaning, what do you do?
Paperback: 978-1-78535-281-2 ebook: 978-1-78535-282-9

Practicing A Course In Miracles
A translation of the Workbook in plain language, with
mentor's notes
Elizabeth A. Cronkhite
The practical second and third volumes of The Plain-Language
A Course In Miracles.
Paperback: 978-1-84694-403-1 ebook: 978-1-78099-072-9

Quantum Bliss

The Quantum Mechanics of Happiness, Abundance, and Health
George S. Mentz
Quantum Bliss is the breakthrough summary of success and
spirituality secrets that customers have been waiting for.
Paperback: 978-1-78535-203-4 ebook: 978-1-78535-204-1

The Upside Down Mountain

Mags MacKean
A must-read for anyone weary of chasing success and happiness
– one woman's inspirational journey swapping the uphill slog for
the downhill slope.
Paperback: 978-1-78535-171-6 ebook: 978-1-78535-172-3

Your Personal Tuning Fork

The Endocrine System
Deborah Bates
Discover your body's health secret, the endocrine system, and
'twang' your way to sustainable health!
Paperback: 978-1-84694-503-8 ebook: 978-1-78099-697-4

Readers of ebooks can buy or view any of these bestsellers by
clicking on the live link in the title. Most titles are published
in paperback and as an ebook. Paperbacks are available in
traditional bookshops. Both print and ebook formats are
available online.
Find more titles and sign up to our readers' newsletter at
http://www.johnhuntpublishing.com/mind-body-spirit
Follow us on Facebook at https://www.facebook.com/OBooks/
and Twitter at https://twitter.com/obooks